THE FATE OF MAN IN THE MODERN WORLD

THE FATE OF MAN
IN THE
MODERN WORLD

by Nicolas Berdyaev

ANN ARBOR PAPERBACKS

THE UNIVERSITY OF MICHIGAN PRESS

First edition as an Ann Arbor Paperback 1961
Copyright © by The University of Michigan 1935
All rights reserved
Published in the United States of America by
The University of Michigan Press and simultaneously
in Toronto, Canada, by Ambassador Books Limited
Translated by Donald A. Lowrie
Manufactured in the United States of America

CONTENTS

CHAPTER I

I

My book, *The End of Our Time*, was written eleven years ago, and four years earlier my *Meaning of History*. In these two books I set forth my historio-sophic ideas in connection with our arrival at the end of a whole historical epoch. Much of what I then prophesied has been fulfilled or is now taking place. But many new elements have arisen which demand consideration, and I feel the need to write a sort of second volume of *The End of Our Time*. More keenly than ever I feel that night and shadow are descending on the world, just as was the case at the beginning of the Middle Ages, before the medieval Renaissance. But stars shine through the night and dawn is coming.

It has become a banality to say that we live in a time of historical crisis, that a whole epoch is ending, and a new one, as yet without a name, is beginning. Some are glad for this, others sorry, but all agree upon the fact. In reality what is

7

happening is something even deeper. We are witnessing a judgment upon not one epoch in history, but upon history itself. And in this sense we live in an apocalyptic time; in this sense only, and not in the sense of the swift arrival of the end of the world. There is such a thing as the internal apocalypse of history. The apocalypse is not merely a revelation of the end of the world : it is also a revelation of the inner events of history, of the internal judgment upon history itself. And this is what is happening now.

Man's existence in this world is an historical existence. Existence is history. Besides this, history is the tragic conflict between the personal and the super-personal or the pre-personal. History never solves the conflict between personality and society, between personality and culture, personality and the mass ; the conflict between quality and quantity. Personality is active in history, within history the individual is revealed, but history is merciless in its attitude toward personality and oppresses the individual. There is a meaning of history, and the recognition of this meaning belongs to Christianity.

At the same time, history is really the failure of man and of culture, the collapse of all human plans. The things man has planned do not come to pass, and the true significance of what takes place escapes man's comprehension. History has never limited itself in the means with which it operates ; it has used any and all means to attain its ends, ends which often remain quite incomprehensible to man, and incommensurate with his own fate. Hegel spoke of the cleverness of the spirit of history, a cleverness which deceives man for the purpose of gaining its own ends. It may be said that in fact the subject of history is not man, not even mankind, but a non-human reason or spirit which in the teaching of Marx is transformed into non-human economics. Marx showed how men are materialized and dehumanized in a capitalist society. History has always worked for the general or universal, rather than for the private or individual. One might say, paradoxically, that man has shown great unselfishness in consenting to history. Perhaps, on the other hand, man was seeking his own interest when he accepted the way of history, but history deceived him, using man's self-seeking as a means to attain quite non-human goals. The cunning of history, against which the living personality rebels ! Man has always been suppressed by history. History was man's destiny, but that destiny never interested history. The incommensurability between history and individual destinies is a tragedy unsolvable within history, a tragedy which demands

the end of history itself. The super-personal
has never been realized in history as a fullness
of personal life. And even when history set
itself personal and human objectives, it realized
them by means of pressure upon the human
personality. Hegel was a sort of incarnation in
thought of the spirit of history, and his philosophy
was thoroughly anti-personal.

Against Hegel and against his idea of a universal spirit, revealing itself in history, men like
Dostoevsky and Kirkegaard rose in protest.
The objectivization of a spirit in history, which
so held the mind of Hegel, really breaks away
from the inner mystery of human existence and
enters the natural-social realm. In such a realm
objects are the given quantities, but not " I "
and " thou," not the world of human existence.
(See my book *Myself and the Objective World*—an
essay on society and solitude.) The failure of
history is none other than the tragedy of the
lack of agreement between what exists as human
and personal on the one hand, and on the other
all objectivization, which is always extra-personal,
non-human, anti-personal and anti-human. Every
objectivization of history is non-human and impersonal. Man is fated to live in two different
orders : that of existence, which is always personal although full of super-personal values, and
that of the objectivized world, always non-

personal and quite indifferent to personal values. Man is always faced with the often fatal dangers arising from the processes which take place in history. He is compelled to realize that the processes of history are fatal, inhuman forces, quite indifferent to his fate, forces as merciless as they are non-human.

We find this merciless non-humanity in the history of the formation of states and empires, in the struggles of tribes and nations, in revolutions and reactions, in wars, in the industrial-capitalistic progress and flowering of states and peoples, in the very formation and development of civilization. Evidently, the means with which history operates, which are used by historic reason, cannot be humanized. It is very difficult, for instance, to humanize the state, that pet creation of history. And at the same time man cannot escape from history, cannot put away his historic destiny. The religious and historic consciousness of Hinduism puts history aside, it is anti-historical. But the life of the Hindu people has not been made happier by that fact. It has lived in terrible poverty and want and in the vast injustice of the caste system, where pariahs are not considered as even human. Christianity is historic : it recognizes the meaning of history and operates in history. The Incarnation took place in history. But Christianity, although it is a historic force and although it has made all Christian nations historic, has never been able to realize itself within history. To objectivize Christianity is to place it in the same category as all objectivity. Objectivized in history, Christianity becomes a social phenomenon, it is subject to the socially prosaic. Christianity accepts history, operates within it, even battles against it, and its spirit would be unrecognizable in an historic objectivization. In a certain sense, every single human soul has more meaning and value than the whole of history with its empires, its wars and revolutions, its blossoming and fading civilizations. And because of this, the break with history is inevitable—a judgment upon history must be passed.

Never before has the conflict been so strongly felt between man and history ; never before have the contradictions of history been so sharply evident; never has man been so at the mercy of the processes at work in history ; at the same time man was never so immersed in history, plunged to its very depths, never so objectivized or so socialized. No single person in modern society is excepted—no one can escape from the sphere of historic events which threaten his very being. In this connection there is no such thing as a privileged group : the fatality of history reduces all to a common level. Man faces the threat that nothing shall be left of himself, of his personal and intimate life, no freedom for his spiritual life or his creative thought. He is submerged in huge collectives, subject to non-human commandments. It is demanded of man that he give himself up without reserve, to society, the state, the race, the class, the nation.

In this connection the world war and the revolutionary processes which have followed it have a metaphysical significance for the fate of man. The very fundamentals of human existence are being shaken. The war was a revelation of the evil, the hatred and jealousy which had been accumulating in mankind : it objectivized the evil which had previously remained hidden, if the expression is permissible, subjective rather than objective. The war revealed the personality of our civilization. It mobilized action, but evil action, rather than good. " Everything for the war." The war was its own sort of communism, of fascism. It cheapened human life, it taught man to take no thought for human life and personality, to consider them as means and instruments in the hands of the fatality of history. And since the war, humanity remains mobilized, it continues to do its military service, it is plunged to the depths in external things : society, the state, nationality, class. Man is made part of the objective world, and is no longer permitted to remain himself, to have his own inner being, to define from within himself his own attitude toward the world and toward other people. And what is still more astonishing is that man in the post-war generations has acquired a taste for all this. He does not feel himself oppressed, he rather inclines to place himself under such a discipline. The war educated a generation of believers in force. The demons of hatred and murder then released continue their activity.

We shall see that in all the present historical process a greater role than that of the war is played by another force, a force of far longer duration, a force of almost cosmic significance : technics [1] and the mechanization of life. The war was the border beyond which there begins a new form of collective human existence, the generalization of mankind. The fact is not of great significance that the process of socializing and nationalizing property and economics is going on so rapidly ; this is a matter of justice and elementary necessity. What is significant is that we are witnessing the socialization and national-ization of human souls, of man himself. This process began with capitalism, in capitalistic

[1] This word, increasingly used in several other languages, stands for the sum of modern scientific progress, especially technical and mechanical : it is the modern "civilization" which some continental people like to contrast with their own "culture."—D. A. L.

industry. The "bourgeoization" of man on the one hand and his "proletarianization" on the other have been fatal for personality, for individual existence. Capitalism is above all anti-personal, the power of anonymity over human life. Capitalism uses man as goods for sale. Everyone agrees that the war was a revelation of a non-brotherly, non-social attitude among men, that it revealed a terrible lack of inner unity, even in the presence of external comradeship and iron discipline. But even without the world war, the bourgeois-capitalist world was a denial of all brotherhood, generality and unity among men. " Man is a wolf to man." The life of the capitalist world is lupine. The war disclosed a complete absence of solidarity and union among men, save the bonds enforced by the discipline of the barracks. It revealed the superficiality of the process of humanization and how thin was the layer of human society which had been really affected by humanizing forces. In the world war and since, there have been active monstrous, organized collectives, beneath which trembles chaos. The war was already a judgment upon history, an immanent judgment upon history itself. It utterly destroyed all illusions : it was a colossal disillusionment in the idealistic under-standing not only of history, but of all high ideals.

II

Once the veil of civilization was torn aside by
the war, the prime realities were revealed in all
their nakedness. The faith in mankind which
had existed for nineteen hundred years was finally
shattered. Faith in God had been shaken earlier,
and loss of one was followed by loss of the other.
The humanist myth about man was exploded, and
the abyss yawned at the feet of mankind. The
wolf-like life of capitalist society was not able to
encourage and support the faith in man. Man
himself is left out of the picture. Economics,
which should have aided man, instead of being for
his service, is discovered to be that for which man
exists : the non-human economic process. The
war merely put into plain words what was already
implicit in capitalism, that man is of no account,
that he has not only ceased to be the supreme
value, but value of any sort. And almost all the
movements launched against capitalism since the
war have accepted the same attitude toward man
which characterized both capitalism and the war
itself. This is the most characteristic process of
our times. Man appears unable to withstand this
process, to defend his own value, to find support
within himself, and he grasps, as at a life-belt, at
the collective, communist or national and racial,
at the State as the Absolute here on earth, or at

organized and technicalized forms of living. Man
has lost his worth; it has been torn to tatters.
Coming out of the war, there have appeared in
the arena of history a series of human collectives,
masses of men who have dropped out of the
organized order and harmony of life, lost the
religious sanctions for their lives and now demand
obligatory organization as the sole means of
avoiding final chaos and degeneration. The
former organic, half-vegetable, life of the mass
has become impossible. All the old religious
sanctions for the power which held great masses
in organic order have vanished : no one believes
in them any more. Every bit of the ancient
prestige of authority has been finally annihilated
in our modern world.

This is not merely a negative process through
which man must pass, in order to get finally upon
his feet and realize his own powers. But it is
noteworthy that at a time when every religious
sanction of authority has vanished, we live in
a very authoritarian epoch. The urge toward
an authoritarian form of life is felt throughout
the whole world : the liberal element seems
completely discredited. But the sanctions for
authority are now different from what they once
were. Authority is born of new collectives, and
these collectives clothe their new leaders with
authority more absolute than was that of the

former anointed monarchs. Chaos has begun to
make itself felt within history. But the source of
chaos is not only in nature, as Tiutchev saw it.
There is the same element in history. Contrasted
with the rationalizing element in history we find
a strong force of the irrational. Lashed by the
chaos of history, buffeted by storms of irrational
forces, wounded by the fatality of history, man
consents to a transition into an era of non-human
existence.

The war was the catastrophic moment which
disclosed that chaos moves beneath the false
civilization of capitalism. The war was chaos,
organized by forced labour. For chaos may
wear an appearance of complete external organization. And since the war, man is not merely
willing, but actively desires to live in the obliga-
torily-organized chaos which expresses itself in
the authoritarian form of life.

The evil and hatred which torment the world
to-day are chaos. An organization which in the
final analysis not only permits, but actually exalts
hatred and evil, can never conquer chaos. True
victory over chaos demands an effort of the spirit,
spiritual change and renaissance. This depends,
not on the fatality of history, not on dark and
irrational forces, but upon human liberty and the
power of Divine grace. But in modern tendencies
in the world we find neither the spirit of freedom

nor the grace of God.   These modern tendencies reveal the terrible loneliness of man.   The tragedy of the situation lies in the fact that great masses of humanity have awakened and come into power at the moment of a falling away from Christianity and the loss of all religious beliefs.

III

The present catastrophe in the world was born, not of a joyful superabundance of creative force, but from man's profound unhappiness, his feeling of hopeless despair.   This may be said, above all, of the national-socialist movement in Germany. The enthusiasm of Nazi youth, which seems actually to exist, is pathological in character, and resembles animation produced by an injection of camphor, rather than the springtime of national life.   The German people are in a state of collective insanity, resulting from the degradation and misfortune to which they have been subject.   But Russian communism also, a different phenomenon, although greatly resembling Naziism in its social morphology, was born not of joy, and not of a surplus of strength, but out of the misfortunes of the war and the injustice of the past.

This element of past misfortunes and unhealthy resentment exists in all revolutions and often distorts their form.   The masses are easily subject to suggestion and often enter a state of collective demoniac possession. They may be possessed only by ideas which permit of a simple and elemental symbolism, a mode quite characteristic of our time. The search for leaders who can lead the masses, offer alleviation for woes, solve all problems, means simply that all the classic authorities have fallen, monarchy and democracy together, and that they must be replaced by new authorities, born of the collective "possession" of the mass. The leader must provide "bread and the theatre." He usually gives more of the latter than the former. Hitler, up to the present moment, has offered almost exclusively the theatre : his politics are like the setting of a Wagnerian opera. He too, by the way, is nourished upon hatred, and it is an astonishing fact that, for a while at least, hatred may be a substitute for bread. For a while men can live on hatred, but not for long. There is more theatre than bread in communist Russia, also, and there also they are trying to live on hatred, hence the constant need of an enemy and the search for " harmers." [1]

[1] " Harmer " or " wrecker " is the word made popular in Soviet Russia to indicate one who does something to impede the progress of the Soviet State. The Vickers engineers were arraigned as " Harmers," but the word applies equally to a peasant who does a poor job of ploughing or a factory workman who is careless in the use of tools.—D. A. L.

Racialism is worse than communism since its ideology includes eternal hatred ; communism, on the other hand, decrees hatred as a way, a method of conflict, while its final ideal proposes the absence of hate. The search for leaders indicates the fall of democracy and decline into Cæsarism, a phenomenon well known in the past. Cæsarism is not a classic political form : it contains elements of decadence. Cæsarism always indicates the end of an epoch, the necessity of passing over to new forms. But what we are witnessing to-day is more than the end of an historical epoch—it is a judgment upon history. The results of the long processes of history have so far advanced in our day that a judgment upon the failures of history is not merely possible but inevitable. These results have been evident in national, political and economic life. They are evident in spiritual culture as well, in literature and philosophy, for even here the true image of man has been disturbed, the integrity of human existence is threatened. And above them all only one positive, creative force reigns—the power of technics.

Man is entering a new cosmos. All the elements of our epoch were present in the past, but now they are generalized, universalized and revealed at last in their true aspect. In these days of the world's agony we feel keenly that

we are living in a fallen world, torn asunder by
incurable contradictions. And it is most notable
that this sense of the world's fallen state is accompanied not by an increased, but by a decreased
sense of sin. This sense of the world's decadence
is strong in Heidegger and his philosophy, or in
Freud or Celine, author of that amazing novel
Voyage au bout de la nuit, but none of them evidence
a consciousness of sin. The decadence of the
world is evident in all modern literature, in
philosophical thought, in political and social life.
Nothing could be moᵣe senseless than modern
economic life with its crises, its over-production,
its unemployment, the power of banks, the
authority of paper fictions, be they in the form
of banknotes, stock certificates or the pages of
a bookkeeper's ledger. There is no security for
life, either material or moral—there is no guar-
anty for anyone, anywhere. We discover that
we are living in a world of crime and phantasms.
The world was all this before, but we have just
now discovered it. Man is threatened on all
sides and does not know what to-morrow will
bring. Modern thinkers like to talk of the
" frontier situation " of man, of the dangers
besetting him on every side (Tillich, Jaspers).
And there is nothing surprising in this, since
history evidently does not undertake to give
man any guarantees of existence or offer any

protection for his life.   History needed man as its material, but has not recognized him as her purpose.

Nowhere is the decadence of our epoch better expressed than in its falsity.   Falsehood has ceased to be recognized as such, and we seem to be in the process of developing a new sort of consciousness in which the differentiation between truth and falsehood is lost.   The world is living in a period of agony which greatly resembles that of the end of antiquity.   But the present situation is more hopeless, since at the close of antiquity Christianity entered the world as a new, young force, while now Christianity, in its human age, is old and burdened with a long history in which Christians have often sinned and betrayed their ideal.   And we shall see that the judgment upon history is also a judgment upon Christianity in history.

The youth of the whole world is seeking a new order, a world-revolution is in progress. But we do not feel the joy of the birth of new life : shadows cover the world.   A cycle of cosmic catastrophes and collapses has begun. But for Christians specially this consciousness brings no despair, and it should not deter us from realizing justice and serving the truth in everyday life.   We are witnessing a return to the first sources, to the final depths.   Christianity is not optimism, but Christian pessimism can be only relative, since beyond the world of unreason and meaninglessness Christianity sees a meaning. The judgment upon history is the voice of reason : it presupposes reason. The inner apocalypse of history is a revelation of the results of not realizing in history the Kingdom of God, *i.e.* Meaning. To accept history is to accept revolution as well. Those who disavow revolution and consider it a crime, forget that to a large degree history is a crime. He who does not approve of crime, should strive for the realization of the Kingdom of God.

CHAPTER II

DEHUMANIZATION

I

THE central theme of our epoch is that of
all history—the fate of man. What is taking
place in the world to-day is not a crisis of humanism (that is a topic of secondary importance), but
the crisis of humanity. We face the question,
is that being to whom the future belongs to be
called man, as previously, or something other?
We are witnessing the process of dehumanization
in all phases of culture and of social life. Above
all, moral consciousness is being dehumanized.
Man has ceased to be the supreme value: he
has ceased to have any value at all. The youth
of the whole world, communist, fascist, national-
socialist or those simply carried away by technics
or sport—this youth is not only anti-humanistic
in its attitudes, but often anti-human. Does this
mean that we should defend the old humanism
against to-day's youth? In many of my books
I have called attention to the crisis in humanism,
and tried to show that it inevitably develops
into anti-humanism and that its final stage is a

denial of man. Humanism has become power-less and must be replaced. Humanism bound up with the renaissance of antiquity is very frail; its development implies an aristocratic social order and democracy has dealt it terrible blows, with the masses and the power of technics breaking into cultural life. The machine de-humanizes human life. Man, desiring no longer to be the image of God, becomes the image of the machine. In its process of democratization, beginning with the eighteenth century, humanism goes along the line of subjecting man to society, to social ordinariness, it generalizes man—it is losing itself.

This democratized and generalized humanism has ceased to be attentive to man: it is interested in the structure of society, but not in man's inner life. This is a fatal and inevitable process. Hence humanism can never be a force capable of withstanding the process of dehumanization. From humanism, which is, after all, a sort of middle-of-the-road humanity, progress is possible in two directions, up or down; toward the idea of the God-man, or toward that of the beast-man. Movement toward super-humanity and the super-man, toward super-human powers, all too often means nothing other than a bestialization of man. Modern anti-humanism takes the form of bestial-ism. It uses the tragic and unfortunate Nietzsche

as a superior sort of justification for dehumanization and bestialization. Few there be who are
moving toward the god-man, " god-humanism "
toward the true super-humanism : many move
toward bestialism, the deification of the bestial.
A bestial cruelty toward man is characteristic of
our age, and this is more astonishing since it is
displayed at the very peak of human refinement,
where modern conceptions of sympathy, it would
seem, have made impossible the old, barbaric
forms of cruelty. Bestialism is something quite
different from the old, natural, healthy barbarism ;
it is barbarism within a refined civilization. Here
the atavistic, barbaric instincts are filtered through
the prism of civilization, and hence they have a
pathological character. Bestialism is a phenomenon of the human world, but a world already
civilized. It does not exist in the animal world,
which belongs to a different degree of being,
with its own significance and justification. The
animals are something much higher than bestial-
ized man. Hence we speak of man's fallen state.
Just now bestialism is set up higher than humanism, as the next degree to which we should
progress. But bestialism at all events is worse
and lower than humanism, although the latter
is powerless to resist it. The bestialism of our
time is a continuation of the war, it has poisoned
mankind with the blood of war. The morals of

war-time have become those of "peaceful" life, which is actually the continuation of war, a war of all against all. According to this morality, everything is permissible : man may be used in any way desired for the attainment of inhuman or anti-human aims. Bestialism is a denial of the value of the human person, of every human personality ; it is a denial of all sympathy with the fate of any man. The new humanism is closing : this is inescapable. But if the end of humanism be held to be the end of humanity, this is a moral catastrophe.

We are entering an inhuman world, a world of inhumanness, inhuman not merely in fact, but in principle as well. Inhumanity has begun to be presented as something noble, surrounded with an aureole of heroism. Over against man there rises a class or a race, a deified collective or state. Modern nationalism bears marks of bestial inhumanity. No longer is every man held to be a man, a value, the image and likeness of God. For often even Christianity is interpreted inhumanly. The " Aryan paragraph " offered to German Christians is the project for a new form of inhumanity in Christianity. But this is nothing very new. Too often in the past Christianity, that is to say Christian humanity, has been inhuman. The old bestialism, naïve, barbarian, instinctive, was not self-conscious ;

it was pre-conscious. But modern bestialism is conscious, deliberate, the product of reflection and civilization, self-justified. Over against the inhumanity of modern nationalism stands that of modern communism. It also refuses to consider every man as of real value, as the likeness and image of God. The class-enemy may be treated as you like. We shall return to this subject later and shall see that nationalism and racialism are worse than communism.

There may have been a time when the image of man, his truly human nature, was not yet revealed —man was in a sort of potential state. This was the case in the past. But now we face something quite different. The image of man has been shaken and has begun to disintegrate after it was revealed. This is going on now in all spheres. Dehumanization has penetrated into all phases of human creativity. In making himself God, man has unmanned himself. This is, of course, a collapse of the humanistic theory of progress. The fate of man is infinitely more complex than it was thought to be in the nineteenth century. The new world which is taking form is moved by other values than the value of man or of human personality, or the value of truth : it is moved by such values as power, technics, race-purity, nationality, the state, the class, the collective. The will to justice is overcome by the will to power.

The dialectic of this process is very delicate. Man desires power, power for himself, but this leads him to put power above self, above man ; it leads him to readiness to sacrifice his own humanity for the sake of power. Power is objectified and drawn away from human existence. Such values as those of technics, the state, the race or the class bestialize man : for the sake of these sorts of power, any desired treatment of the individual is permitted.

It would be a mistake to think that modern bestialism and its attendant dehumanization are based upon the triumph of base instincts and appetites and a denial of all the values ordinarily held to be idealistic. Modern bestialism and dehumanization are based upon idolatry, the worship of technics, race or class or production, and upon the adaptation of atavistic instincts to this worship. We have already noted that modern barbarism is a civilized barbarism. The war aroused ancient instincts—racial and national : the instincts of power and violence, instincts of revenge, but all these are now realized in the forms of technical civilization. In reality we are witnessing a return of the human mass to the ancient collective with which its history began ; the return to a state which preceded the development of personality. But this ancient collective takes on civilized forms and uses the technical instruments of civilization. Keyserling sees this "world-revolution" as the uprising of tellurian forces, the Earth opposing the Spirit. But telluric forces are natural, cosmic, while the forces of to-day are those of technical civilization.

In modern tendencies the influence of two thinkers of the nineteenth century is very strongly felt—the influence of Marx and Nietzsche. They signify the end and the destruction of humanism. Marx and Nietzsche are in conflict for the control of the world. The influence of Nietzsche upon fascism and national-socialism is unmistakable. His influence is felt in the modern apotheosis of a powerful leader, and in the development of a cruel type of youth devoid of all sympathy with suffering. Nietzsche himself, that solitary aristocratic thinker, would turn away in horror from the social results of his preaching. Nietzsche did not like the idea of Pan-Germanism, he was not a German nationalist and would probably suffer pangs of disgust at the modern plebeian spirit, devoid of all traits of nobility.

But influence works that way, in the subterranean and subconscious sphere, and often arouses forces which it was far from the thought of the creative mind to set in motion. The historical influence of Luther, for instance, moved in quite a different direction from that which he intended. Luther never thought that protestantism

would become rationalistic and moralistic. The
influence of Marx on communism is apparently
developing much more as he intended, but still
the Russian communist revolution would doubt-
less greatly surprise him, since it quite contra-
dicts or even renounces his teaching. At the
moment the influence of Marx and Nietzsche is
active in the direction of the dehumanization of
society and culture. And this dehumanization
is at the same time de-christianization. Conservative Christians rarely note how completely this is
true. They are inclined to think that humanism
was a de-christianization, and for some reason
they do not associate dehumanization with the
fact that the image of God in man is being
darkened, that man is losing the sense, which
Christianity revealed to him, of being a son of
God.

In the cultural and ideal tendencies of our
epoch dehumanization moves in two directions,
toward naturalism and toward technicism. Man
is subject either to cosmic forces or to technical
civilization. It is not enough to say that he
subjects himself : he is dissolved and disappears
either in cosmic life or else in almighty technics ;
he takes upon himself the image, either of nature
or of the machine. But in either case he loses
his own image and is dissolved into his component
elements. Man as a whole being, as a creature

centred within himself, disappears ; he ceases to
be a being with a spiritual centre, retaining his
inner continuity and his unity.   To the fractional
and partial elements of man there is offered not
only the right to autonomy, but to supremacy in
life.   The self-assertion of these disunited elements in man, as, for instance, the non-sublimated
elements of the subconscious, sexual desire, or
the will to dominance and power, bear witness to
the fact that the unified, whole image of man is
disappearing and giving place to non-human and
natural elements.   Man has disappeared ; there
remain only certain of his functions.

This dissolution of man into certain functions
is the product, first of all, of technical civilization.   The process of dehumanization attains its
climax in the technique of modern war, where
human bravery is no longer necessary.   Technical
civilization demands that man shall fulfil one or
another of his functions, but it does not want
to reckon with man himself—it knows only his
functions.   This is not dissolving man in nature,
but making him into a machine.   When civilized
man yearns for nature, he is longing to return to
wholeness and unconsciousness, since consciousness has shaken his unity and made him unhappy.
This is romanticism.   Klages is a good example
of this attitude.   When man strives for complete
fulfilment of his technical functions, when he

tries to be like his new god, the machine, the tendency is just the opposite to that noted above : not toward wholeness, integrity, but toward greater and greater differentiation. But man disappears in both these tendencies, both dehumanize him. Man cannot be the image either of nature or of the machine. Man is the image and likeness of God. The formation of man as an integral being, as a personality, that process which began in the world of the Bible and the Greek world, was finished only in Christianity. Now we are witnessing a sort of reverse cosmic process, against not only Christianity, but against the Bible and against Greek culture. Modern neo-classicism is deadly formalism, and without life or power.

The process of dehumanization is specially notable in modern literature, particularly in the novel. If we consider two of the most prominent French novelists, Proust and André Gide, we cannot fail to remark that in their works man is decomposed, that a whole image no longer exists, that there are only elements of sensation and intellectual or rational states. First of all the heart disappears, as the central and integral organ of the human being, as the bearer of human feelings. Man mourns, even to despair, at this loss of the integral human being, but he is powerless to regain it. Occasionally he even rejoices at his own elimination. These novels no longer contain a wealth of human types, the multifarious human world, but only fragments and elements of that being which once was called man. The modern psychological novel, talented and refined, is concerned with the analysis of the subconscious, is plunged into the uncertain world of sensations, is terribly complex, from the intellectual point of view. Man is resolved into some of his component elements under the power of the subconscious and the rationalistic. Modern novelists almost completely lack creative imagination, they are either preoccupied with themselves or simply picture the evil realities with which they are burdened. This is the case, for instance, with Celine. The creative gift of transfiguration is disappearing from art.

Even the rare novelists who concern themselves with the metaphysical or the mystical, as for example Jouhandeau, are oppressed by demoniac powers such as even Dostoevsky knew not; Dostoevsky who saw in every man the image of God, who perceived light in the deepest shadow. Malraux's characters disappear beneath their sadistic instincts. In the works of Lawrence, man as an integral being is lost in the mystical elements of sex; man becomes a function of sex, instead of sex being a function of man. This is not pornography, it is a reflection of the same

dehumanizing process now going on in the
world, expressed with great artistic talent. Huxley
pictures a varied human world, but a world in
disintegration, where the true image of man is
hard to discover. Compare the modern novelist
with Dickens, for example. The distance novels
have travelled since then is surprising—it is as
though some cosmic catastrophe had taken place.
In Dickens we find a richly varied human world,
a world of truly human types and images, tremendous power and great creative imagination. Man
is still himself, he retains his own image, even
when he is comic or really bad. In the genial
Pickwick Club, which has in it somewhat of
Cervantes, the purely human world is still intact,
man's true image remains. The same surprising
difference is observed in comparing the modern
novel with those of Balzac or Leo Tolstoy. In
Tolstoy we find a strong element of the cosmic,
but the integral and varied world of humanity,
not yet decomposed, is still preserved in the
midst of cosmic forces and elements. Nothing
of the sort can be discovered in the novels of
to-day, although the modern novels contain much
of perfect truth about man and what is happening
to him in the present age.

The process of dehumanization is evident in
modern science as well, in the sense that science
reveals phases of natural life which are not con-

nected with the natural milieu to which man is habituated. Physics has revealed sounds that we cannot hear and colours we cannot see. And the technical results of modern physics place man in a new and untried sphere, a non-humanized, cosmic milieu. Physics takes pride in its completely ex-centric attitude toward man. The breath-taking achievements of modern technics are connected with the great discoveries of modern physics. That modern technics are dehumanizing man and turning him into a mere technical function is clear to everyone, and, as I pointed out in my article " Man and the Machine," this is everywhere recognized.

When we turn to the question of dehumanization in philosophic thought, we find a more complex process. This process has long been going on in philosophy : it was evident in empiricism, in idealism, in positivism, in philosophic naturalism and materialism. But at the same time modern creative philosophy is a reaction against these processes. Philosophy has always sought the meaning of things—it could never be content with meaninglessness. Hence philosophy now puts the question, more sharply than ever before, of man and of human existence. The so-called existential philosophy is seeking to discover the structure of being in human existence, but even here the integral image

of man disappears.   In this regard Heidegger is
most interesting.   Being, as worry, fear, prosaicness, death, is being revealed in fallen and unfortunate human existence.   But man himself is
lost behind this fear, this care, this death.   Worry
turns out to be more significant than the man
who worries.   Man is constructed out of worries,
just as human existence is built up from death.
The philosophy of Heidegger is a philosophy of
nothing.   Nothing is non-existent.   This is an
ontology of nothing as the final mystic secret
of being, a philosophy of despair, absolute
pessimism.   This type of philosophy is characteristic of our times.   The same motives,
although in softened forms, may be seen in
Jaspers.   The melancholy and tragic Kirkegaard
is now exerting on modern philosophy an influence toward an ontology of nihilism, which is
not found in Kirkegaard himself.   Immersion
in human existence, instead of revealing man,
shows forth his decomposition and decay.   What
metaphysics there is in Freud is a metaphysic of
death and nothingness.   The only instinct higher
than that of sex, and capable of being set over
against it, is the instinct of death.

But even in modern European religious and theological thought this process of dehumanization
is evident, although here it has a different significance.   Karl Barth with his dialectic theology

is the dehumanization of Christianity. This
mode of thought discovers in the creative world
only sin and powerlessness. There remains a
fervent faith in God, but in a God absolutely
transcendent, separated by an abyss from the
world and from man. The image of God in
man is shattered. The Word of God is the only
connection between God and creation and for
man there remains only the possibility of hearken-
ing to God's word. Here we glimpse the influence of Kirkegaard in a different direction. Just
as is the case with Heidegger, Karl Barth's world
and his humanity are godless, but God remains.
This is a passionate reaction against humanism
in Christianity which has resulted in a degradation or even a denial of man. Thomism, so
powerful in the Catholic world, seeks to maintain a Latin balance and equality; it remains
optimistic, and we discover in it elements of that
old humanism which dates back to the medieval
renaissance. In Thomism man is not denied, he
is merely diminished : man is regarded as an
insignificant being, possessing neither real freedom, nor creative capacities ; he is a second-rate
being. Thomism is also a reaction against the
humanism of our modern age. It also contains
elements of dehumanization hidden behind the
conflict with all modernism in religious and
philosophical thought. But most powerful of

all are the elements of dehumanization in the life of modern society and the modern state.

II

Freedom in social life presents a paradox which gives rise to a whole series of contradictions. We are living in an epoch of the acute contradictions of freedom. In the political and the economic spheres, freedom is passing through a degenerate form. The principles which once were revered as the assurances of liberty have lost their power and no longer inspire mankind. The principles of the French Revolution have been outlived. Modern youth is no longer interested even in the ideology of Liberalism or that of democracy. Formal democratic parliamentarism has compromised itself; it suffers from an inertia so terrible that it is evidently incapable of reforming society.

The freedom of the spirit is a sacred symbol whose significance cannot be limited by a given time or by the changing forms of a given epoch. Nevertheless, freedom in social, political or even cultural life has lost its power to inspire, men have cooled toward it; they no longer believe in it. We are living in an epoch of the decadence of liberty. Liberty has become a deceiver. It has become a principle of Conservativism, and not seldom has it been used to conceal human slavery. The purely formal comprehension of liberty has led to actual non-liberty. Liberty has been proclaimed, but has been found impossible to realize by the greater part of mankind. Economic freedom especially has proved to be a mockery of man's real freedom. The rights of man and of the citizen have been completely discredited. They have gone the way of the atomistic world-view of the eighteenth century, of the French Revolution, of the individualism of outworn Liberalism and the decadent forms of democracy. If there is an eternal element in democracy, by the way, it is surely connected, not with the idea of the supremacy of a nation, but with the idea of the subjective rights of human personality, with freedom of spiritual life, freedom of conscience, thought, speech and creativity.

This idea of inalienable subjective rights for the human personality derives, not from Rousseau nor from the French Revolutionary Jacobins, but from Christianity and the movements connected with the Reformation. But the idea of the rights of man was distorted and perverted in the bourgeois-capitalistic society of the nineteenth and twentieth centuries; although given new impetus by the French Revolution, it was distorted in the formal bourgeois democracy which followed. And this is connected with the very

fundamentals of a world-view, a *Weltanschauung*.
The Spanish philosopher Ortego remarks very
wittily that the idea of Liberalism as freedom of
personality from the power of the state or of
society is rooted not at all in the French Revolution and not in the principles of democracy,
but in feudalism, in the medieval castle whose
knight-proprietor defended it with sword in
hand.   There is much truth in this : personality
must defend itself against the absolute power of
the state or of society.   Very often thinkers fail
to understand that the real problem is not that
of arriving at an organization of society and the
state under which these two would grant freedom
to human personality, but rather the problem of
confirming the freedom of the personality against
the unlimited authority of society and the state.
This means that true freedom of personality has
a spiritual rather than a social origin ; it is defined
by its being rooted in the spiritual rather than
the social world.

   True liberty cannot be founded upon the view
of sociological positivism which proclaims society
as the supreme reality and the source of all the
life of man.   But European democracy rests
upon just this sociological positivism.   Durgk-
heim was the herald of a genuine sociological
religion.   The proclamation of the rights of man
and of the citizen was a statement of the rights

of a member of society, of the citizen of a state, rather than of a man as an integral being, a free spirit. The emphasis upon man as a citizen covered and obscured the concept of man as a free spirit belonging to another order of being, and on the other hand it obstructed the vision of man as a labourer and producer. The right of every man to worthy existence by his own labour was somehow not proclaimed. The contradictions and the false results of this proclamation of the rights and liberties of the citizen in a bourgeois society have called forth a reaction against the idea of freedom for human personality itself. The rights of the individual have been confined to the formal and political and do not extend into the economic sphere where freedom to labour under the capitalist regime has been a mockery of man's true freedom. Liberty was discovered to be protection of the rights of the strong, leaving the weak defenceless. This is one of the paradoxes of liberty in social life. Freedom turned out to be freedom for oneself and slavery for others. He is the true lover of liberty who desires it for others as well as for himself. Liberty has become the protection of the rights of a privileged minority, the defence of capitalistic property and the power of money. The vast masses of labour have not known liberty. The right to vote for a parliament is

sheer mockery of the poverty-stricken condition
and the slavery of great masses of men.   Freedom
has created monstrous injustices.   And men have
ceased to love freedom when they have become
conscious of their right to a more worthy and
more active existence.   In formal democracies
freedom has become an obstacle in the way of
social reform, and now men have desired dictators, for the purpose of achieving such reform.
Dynamic liberty is not formal freedom of choice :
dynamic liberty presupposes a previous choosing
of the truth.

The natural reaction against this distorted
freedom in liberal democracies has developed into
a reaction against the eternal truth of a free human
spirit.   The most liberal of democracies have
never known the spiritual bases of freedom, and
the movements now directed against democracy
have no desire to know them.   Liberalism has
separated the citizen from the integral personality.
It has separated rights from responsibilities.   For
in the final analysis freedom is not only rights, it
is duties as well.   God has laid upon man the
duty of being free, of safeguarding freedom of
spirit, no matter how difficult that may be, or how
much sacrifice and suffering it may require.   And
man is obligated to respect and regard the freedom
of his fellow-man, not only his own.   There are
too many lovers of their own liberty in the world.

These include all Communists, all Fascists, all National-Socialists and all others possessed by the demon of the will to power. And they all deny the liberty of their fellow-man. The petrifaction of freedom in liberal democracies has come about just because freedom was comprehended only individually (not personally) and was often interpreted as meaning "leave me in peace." Freedom meant that each retired within himself, into his own family, or individual economic interests, or his own business enterprise. Freedom as it is understood in France has become a conservative principle, the defence of the *status quo*. Granted such a conception of freedom, every slightly radical change in society is inevitably regarded as violence.

Freedom is the eternal basis of the human spirit—the spirit is freedom. Freedom is the eternal basis of human intercourse : to be true communion it must be free. But the eternal basis of liberty cannot be attached to changing political forms such as Liberalism and democracy. The problem of freedom is vastly deeper than that of liberalism. Liberty has no permanent foundations in Liberalism. In principle democracy subordinates the individual personality to the nation. This is why the liberal-democratic principles are powerless to defend liberty against the incursions upon it by the communists and

fascists of to-day.   Formal Liberalism, indifferent
to the truth and to individualism, has not only
led to terrible injustice and inequality, but it has
given to the idea of freedom associations which
are now repulsive and unpleasant.   Liberty must
not be understood in a negative and formal sense
only, but rather in its positive content.   Liberty
will be saved by its union with Truth—it can not
be saved by indifference to Truth.   Know the
Truth and the Truth shall make you free.   The
age of sceptical liberty is closing, a new age is
beginning.   Freedom, understood as something
positive and joined with creativeness, becomes
creative energy.   Freedom means not only freedom of choice, but choice itself.   Freedom
cannot be simply a formal self-defence ; it must
lead to creative activity.   The transition is inevitable from formal liberty, by which each
protects and defends himself, to true freedom by
means of which human society is creatively transfigured.   But the transition to true and creative
liberty means, first of all, not the rights of the
citizen, but of man as a concrete and integral
being, a being rooted in the spiritual order.

The transition to true freedom also means the
proclamation of the rights of the labourer, the
producer.   Winning true liberty for every producer, every labourer, means the abolition of
that social order which was based on so-called

" economic freedom," an order which made every man a wolf to his fellows. This is to say that liberty in social life is a paradox, that it easily transposes into its opposite and becomes distorted into a conditional falsehood. Modern movements under the sign of the crisis of liberty feel this very keenly. The socialists have all along criticized the formal liberty of liberal democracy, refusing to accept it as a true guarantee of freedom for the labouring class. Modern tendencies, even those quite hostile to Socialism, have borrowed very much from it, without acknowledgement. In the liberal democratic states we see the development of a thirst for gain, the worship of the golden calf, dishonesty and the acceptance of bribes. In the dictatorial states, fascist or communist, there is a development of thirst for power and violence, a desire for bloodshed and cruelty.

This crisis and decadence of liberty, so characteristic of our epoch, puts to social philosophy the question of liberty on a new and more fundamental level. But people who are carried along on the currents of our time are not conscious of this new face on the problem. It has not been recognized, either, by those who once considered themselves the defenders of liberty. The real meaning of liberty is absent from both sides of the present conflict between aging Liberalism and

the partisans of an authoritarian state. Liberalism
is exclusively a social philosophy : the liberals
are social-minded and for them liberty means
only a form of political organization for society,
whereby society grants certain subjective rights
to its citizens.   Liberalism is a one-planed world-
concept : it fails to see that man belongs to two
planes of being.   This means that there is not
only such a thing as freedom in society, but
freedom from society as well, a freedom which is
based on something quite other than society.
The so-called subjective rights of man do not
arise from society.   Freedom of the spirit does
not depend on any kind of social organization.
Liberty is a limitation of the authority of society
over personality, the power of the State over man.
It implies no specific form of organization, social
or national, but only that man belongs to another
plane of being, to the realm of the spirit.   Liberty
is spirit and the spirit is liberty, and just because
of this, liberty is reduced and diluted in the degree
to which it lowers itself to the plane of the
material.   Maximum liberty exists for spiritual
life, for human thought and conscience, for the
intimate life of the personality.   Liberty in
political life is already a reduced and imperfect
form.   And the minimum liberty should be given
in economic life, since this is nearest to the
material and furthest from the spirit.

The very possibility of human life on the earth depends upon economics and it would appear impossible to leave to chance a matter which might condemn man to death by starvation. Even in the life of the individual there is greater freedom in the life of the spirit and less in the purely physiological. The material must be organized, it cannot be given a liberty which amounts to leaving it to blind chance. But so great is the perversion of the hierarchy of values in human life that no freedom is granted the spirit, while for the material full liberty is offered. At a time when freedom of thought and speech and spiritual creativeness was desired, great freedom was accorded to economics. The material appetites and lusts made orgy, they exploited and crowded the weak and dependent, while the spirit was cramped and oppressed. This is of course a vivid evidence of the decadence of the world. At the present time there are voices crying for the organization of material, the regulation of economics, but they propose the same methods of regulation and organization for the spirit which they use for economic life. They want to treat the spirit just as they do the material. This leads to a dictatorship of world-outlook, a dictatorship over the spirit. This is evidenced in Communism as in Fascism, and still more in National-Socialism. It is a monism in which rules applicable only to the material are applied to spirit as well. This is materialism, open or disguised. Even those who are defending liberty against a dictated philosophy are far more interested in liberty for their material appetites than in liberty of the spirit or of conscience, and this still further compromises the idea of freedom. Man is reduced to a one-plane being, and this one-plane being is organized by one method. In such a one-plane organization, material always triumphs over spirit.

This tyrannic, one-plane attitude is not a new thing, revealed for the first time in Communism and Fascism: we have far earlier examples. The idea existed first of all in all the old theocratic systems which envisaged theophanies in relative social forms, historically variable. This is almost universally recognized. But it is interesting to discover the same "one-plane-ness" which leads to the imprisonment of the spirit and to tyranny, even if in a disguised form—to discover the same thing in the ideology of democracy, in J. J. Rousseau, in the Jacobins. Jacobin democracy knows no limitations for the protection of personal liberty or the independence of the spirit. Rousseau did not recognize freedom of conscience. He believed in an obligatory religion for all citizens and proposed to exile Christians from his perfect republic. This is a new form of the same principle which was in the Utopia of Plato, and in medieval theocracy. The Jacobin democracy undertakes to organize the spirit by the same methods as those by which it organizes the material. Democracy, too, turns toward a sort of etatism, the absoluteness of the state. In France to-day considerable freedom exists, bound up with all the cultural treasure of the French people, joined to a respect for the dignity of human personality. But the radical party, dominant in France, and uniting itself to the Jacobin tradition, also professes one form of etatism : it is a party of a definite world-view and would have the state educate its people in it. But this too is ideocracy, a softened and modified form of the dictatorship of a world-view. It will always be thus, when man is held to be a creature of only one plane, when he is considered as a social entity only, determined exclusively by society and the state. That is to deny man's self-being and the independence of his life on the plane of the spiritual.

Christianity reveals and confirms man's belonging to two planes of being, to the spiritual and to the natural-social, to the Kingdom of God and the Kingdom of Cæsar. Christianity affirms that man belongs at once to the realm of liberty and that of necessity, and maintains that these two are incommensurate and incapable of complete fusion.

But we are living in an age when the Christian revelation and the freedom of the spirit are renounced, and man is handed over to the temptations of the Grand Inquisitor. Even Christianity has been touched by these temptations, but at the moment it seems to be freeing and cleansing itself from their influence, at a time when the rest of the world lies completely in their power. Everything is so tangled and confused that great clarity of spirit and of vision is necessary if one would distinguish rightly among the images presented by our modern world. One of the most confusing elements in the picture of division and recombination is that of liberty, threatened on all sides, defended by the partisans of the bourgeois-capitalist world. But even in the presence of the most complete civic and political freedom, men may be deprived of freedom of the spirit, of conscience, freedom of creativeness : they may be deprived of personality and originality, as concerns their contact with the basic elements of spiritual life. Men may be in economic slavery, bereft of economic freedom, if such freedom is conceived not as the right to sell one's labour, not the right to exploit one's neighbour and leave great masses of men in poverty and bitter dependence, but as liberty to realize a worthy human existence.

In the capitalist world freedom has been the

privilege of a few, and a doubtful privilege even for them, since the existence of the very exploiters was itself a nightmare existence, in its turn exploited and oppressed. The crisis of capitalism is the crisis of liberty. But if liberty is of a false or fictitious sort, it should be overthrown. In that case its overthrow would clear the way for true and actual liberty. The world is caught, just now, between this sort of false, decomposing liberty on the one hand, and the complete denial of liberty, the dictated world-view, on the other. This dictated world-view differs from that of the Middle Ages in that the medieval world-view was something truly integral, organic, grandiose, while that of to-day is something hastily tacked together, ill-considered and lacking all depth. The *Weltanschauungen* of to-day are conditional symbols or myths which the demagogues use to control the masses with. This is the state of things in our world to-day.

Freedom of labour, as proclaimed in the societies of the nineteenth and twentieth centuries, started out by being the exploitation of labour; it has now become the freedom of the unemployed. It is a clear expression of the contradictions and paradoxes of liberty in social life. Marx did not foresee these results of industrial-capitalist development. He imagined that the quantity of labourers would automatically

increase in a capitalist society, that the proletariat would become even more numerous,
would be a united and disciplined force which
was called to create a new social order. He
noted the exploitation of labourers, but failed to
see their transformation into the unemployed.
What has actually happened is that with the
technicalization and rationalization of industry,
the number of labourers decreases, man-power
is replaced by the machine, and instead of an
increase in the number of workers we have an
increase in the number of all sorts of function-
aries of industrial bureaucracy. This changes
the whole perspective. Labour never was free.
Human culture and society has always been built
upon the slavery of the working-class. Labour,
hard physical toil, is the Biblical curse laid upon
man. At first labour was slavery, then serfdom,
and it became " free " in capitalist society only
in the sense that it has become an article of trade
which may be " freely " sold under threat of
starvation. Even in the communist society of
present-day Russia, labour has become serfdom
since it is commandeered and cruelly exploited
by the state in the person of the communist
bureaucracy.

A new form of the enslavement of labour is
arising in the modern authoritarian states, based
upon a dictated world-view. This is a sur-

prising process. The social milieu becomes more unified, but in this very unification personality is more heavily oppressed than in a more differentiated society. Instead of the living personality of the worker, his welfare, the rights of labour, we see proclaimed as the supreme value the power and well-being of the state, the social collective. The means of production, instead of being given to the producers, as Marx demanded, are turned over to the fascist or communist state. The State is recognized as the subject, while man becomes the object. This is the extreme form of the objectivization of human existence : man is emptied of every inner value. The process of socializing economic life, a process not only just but necessary, now becomes a process of socializing integral humanity, that is, the subjection of man to society in the most secret and intimate spheres of his being.

But this process is just the reverse of that needed to produce a true brotherhood of man, the communion of personalities, of " me " and " thee." All men become the objects of organization. The crisis through which mankind is passing, the denial of liberty is the denial of man himself. For the truly justified process of reducing mankind to a level may proceed in two directions : it may proclaim the dignity, the value and the liberty of every individual because in him there is seen the image of God, or the existence of this image may be denied, and with it all freedom and value of the individual man. Either the privileges of the nobility may be extended to all mankind, raising all to the level of nobility, since human dignity was first recognized for the aristocracy, or all men may be deprived of these privileges and transformed into an enslaved proletariat. We may conceive either a general aristocratization of human society, or a general democratization which would mean lowering the level of all human qualities. At the moment the process is evidently moving in the latter direction, and hence the problem of society is above all the problem of man. The anthropological question strikes deeper than the purely sociological.

At the time of the Renaissance the freedom of human thought was proclaimed, but the dialectic of that emancipatory process led to the transformation of freedom of thought into " freethought." This is a new dogma quite different from freedom of thought. " Free-thought " has proved to be a compression or even a denial of man's spiritual life. And true freedom of thought will confirm, not free-thought, but the truth of Christianity. The emancipation did not set free the whole man, it simply liberated thought itself, as a sphere quite apart from human existence: it was the declaration of autonomy for thought, not for man himself. This autonomy was proclaimed in all spheres of social and cultural life, and everywhere it brought about the dissociation of these various phases of life from the integral man. The autonomy of economic life, for instance, created the fatal figure of the "economic man" who is really no man at all. The crisis and decline of the freedom of thought is in direct causal relation with the fact that it is not so much man's thought which is set free, as that thought has been set free from man, has become autonomous. But this autonomy is something quite different from freedom.

By the same token, the autonomy of the moral law is not the freedom of man. Here we find the roots of the processes now at work in the world. All the various autonomies, that of thought, which has become the dogma of "free-thought," the autonomy of economics, which has been transformed into capitalism, the autonomy of morals, now become dead legalism— all forget man himself, his true integrity. And the modern denial of liberty, of man himself, cannot be overcome by the autonomies of thought, of morals and of economics, for these are the very causes of the modern denial of liberty. The only thing which can stand against all these processes is integral man himself, with his feet

set in the spiritual order.   Man should proclaim
not formal liberty, but true freedom for the very
content of human existence.   This is the struggle
for human quality, for human worth, for true
aristocratization.   But this involves the great
difference between the concepts of freedom held
by Liberalism and by Christianity.   Liberalism
demands a formal liberty and is quite indifferent
to truth or to the content of human life.   Christianity demands liberty as the very essence of
Christian truth, as the qualitative content of all
human life.   And this distinction is valid for
thought, for cultural creativity, for social and
economic life.   The autonomy of economic life
in capitalism has been the same sort of dehumanization as the autonomy of thought in sceptical
" free-thought."

Formal freedom of thought led to free-thinking
and scepticism.   Decline and degeneration lead
to the demand for dictatorship, not only in
economic and political life, but to a dictatorship
in thought and philosophy which is nothing less
than the denial of freedom of the spirit.   Taken
by itself, this demand for dictatorship and leader-
ship has its good element : it is akin to the
significance which the one-person idea has in
political life, *i.e.* men of creative initiative, powerful enough to take responsibility upon themselves.   Without this type of person, reform of

any sort is impossible. Left alone, the democratic element becomes inert and conservative—it must of necessity be combined with the aristocratic and monarchial, not in the sense of a monarchy, but of one person, like a president or other leader with real power. But this does not at all imply a dictated world-view.

It is amazing that the modern dictatorship of ideas is not at all connected with real spiritual unity and with some world-view which actually exists, and with which the masses are as saturated as in the past they were impregnated with the Christian faith. Unity of belief is dictated by the authority of the state. The state feels the need of creating a spiritual unity, the need to unify its whole human constituency. It is absurd to think that the whole popular mass in Russia is penetrated by Marxian theory, or that in Germany by the racial theories of Gobineau and Chamberlain. A dictatorship must create a unity of ideas. In this connection Communism is better off than most dictatorships, since the Marxian theory exists and offers a real system of thought which can be adopted. Fascism not so well off. The modern dictatorship of ideas is based on the assumption that the spiritual life may be dealt with on exactly the same basis as the material life, that the spirit and thought and the creativeness of culture are susceptible to the same sort of organization as political or economic life. But this always means that spirit is considered as an epiphenomenon, that its primacy over the material is denied. In practice, the process of organizing a unity of thought usually leads to strengthening the police and espionage organs of the state. The desire to do away with spiritual and mental anarchy, and to attain a spiritual unity and an integral world-view, is a desire quite just and deserving of our sympathy : the age of formal Liberalism, of scepticism and free-thinkers, is approaching the end of its road. But along the way there lie in wait the temptations of the Grand Inquisitor. One of these is the dictated world-view. It has led to the most evil results in Russian Communism and in German National-Socialism. The dictated *Weltanschauung* is not a real elimination of chaos, but only a formal organization of chaos, a superficial, despotic order beneath which chaos never ceases to yawn. The modern movements in this direction have tremendous symptomatic significance : they mean transition into a new epoch, but they do not mean that epoch itself. Their positive value is biological, first of all, as indicative of the vital force of modern youth, its capacity for enthusiasm.

III

Both Russian Communism and Fascism, as modern phenomena are by-products, after-effects of the war. Fascism, besides being a war-baby, is also a reaction against Communism, and its emotional bases are less positive and creative than negative and reactionary. German Fascism, National-Socialism, was born of the misfortunes and deprivations of the German people. Both Communism and Fascism, much alike in their social morphology, justly protest against the degeneration of formal liberty which means scepticism, unbelief and indifference to the truth. But instead of proceeding to the true freedom of man, as an integral being, a spiritual nature, as producer and citizen, they proceed to both formal and actual denial of liberty. From the oppression of human personality in a capitalist economy or the a-personalism and inhumanity of the war or of the state, they proceed to the unification of the same oppression and extend it over the whole race. This is merely a continuation of the same process of dehumanization and depersonalization which has been noted above. Freedom and personality are denied, not in some special "bourgeois" sense, as is so often claimed by modern demagogues, but in their eternal, spiritual sense. Man is being betrayed. He has ceased to be the supreme value : he has been replaced by values which are really beneath him in the scale. Our epoch faces the question of whether man shall continue to exist, or be replaced by quite another being, produced by class and social, or racial and national training.

There is a difference between Italian Fascism and German Naziism in both style and symbolism. The Italian Fascism is based upon the symbol and myth of the state as the higher being and the supreme value; it strives to continue the Roman tradition and is classic in style. In fact it is much better, much less tyrannous, than German National-Socialism, although its deification of the state is a patent return to paganism. German National-Socialism is based upon the symbol and myth of the race as a higher form of being and the supreme value. It loves to talk of the spirit of the German people, of the earth, of the mystical significance of blood : its style is romantic. The state is only an instrument in the hands of nationality and the race. But this touches the inner being of man far more vitally than the fascist ideology of the state. The development of a pure and powerful race becomes a maniacal, pathological idea, something which demands a psycho-analysis of the whole people which has fallen into a state of collective insanity and demoniac possession.

It may be said in passing, that the other nations of Europe who consider themselves more healthy and sane, have little right to pass judgment upon the Germans, since international policies, the Treaty of Versailles, the self-seeking of each nation under the guise of the best interests of Europe—all these are much to blame for the unfortunate state of the German people to-day. It must also be noted that in spite of their thoroughly unhealthy nature, both Fascism and Naziism contain some positive values. Among such we may note the sound criticism of formal political democracy which is living through a mortal crisis, in the desire to set up a real corporative or syndical representation, truly representing the economic and professional interests of the people, in the elimination of party conflicts and even in the necessity of a powerful authority for social reform or the appeal to direct action arising from popular life, as contrasted with the indirect action presented in a fictitious party representation in the sphere of parliament. This is a transition from formal social realism. That old socialist, Mussolini, who now cannot bear the sound of the word, is nevertheless at present engaged in working out a very radical socialist programme, and will probably see it realized. The Socialism of the Nazis is much less certain, in spite of their retention of the word. This merely shows the relative use of words in modern social life. Up to the present moment Hitler has done almost nothing for social reform, and is even, to judge by appearances, compelled to rely upon financial and capitalist groups. Still there are some positive social-economic elements in the national-socialist programme.

It has become quite usual to contrast Fascism with democracy. The battle against Fascism is to be waged in the name of democratic principles. This is a very superficial attitude. Democracy may not be considered as something static; we must penetrate into the dynamic of democracy. Fascism is one of the extreme results of democracy, a revelation of its dialectic. Fascism sets itself up against a liberal-parliamentarian democracy, rather than democracy in general. In his book on the principles of Fascism, Mussolini says definitely that Fascism is democracy, but democracy of an authoritarian sort. This may sound paradoxical and may shock the adepts of old forms of democracy, still it may be affirmed that Fascism is one of the results of J. J. Rousseau's doctrine of the sovereignty of the people. The doctrine of popular sovereignty, which seems to be implied in the word democracy, of itself gives no guarantee of liberty for human personality. Rousseau believed that the common will of a sovereign people was holy and infallible, which gave rise to the myth he created, like that of Marx concerning the infallibility and sanctity of the will of the proletariat.

In reality, however, a sovereign people, just like a sovereign proletariat, may abolish all liberty and completely suppress human personality, may demand that man renounce his personal conscience. In complete control of the state, a sovereign people may take its state for a church and on that basis begin to organize the spirit and spiritual life. And every "ideocracy," whose prototype is the Republic of Plato, takes the state for a church and ascribes ecclesiastical functions to the state. In principle the Jacobin democracy is already a tyrannical ideocracy denying the freedom of the spirit. The idea of inalienable subjective rights for personality is of quite a different origin, and is, of course, much more Christian than that of a sovereign people. As Mussolini remarks, when a united people takes the state finally into its own hands, the state actually becomes that of the people. Then the state becomes absolute, it is subject to no limitations whatever. Against an absolute state, oppressed personality has always struggled, the personality of subject-groups such as the bourgeoisie, the intellectuals, the workers, and they have tried to enforce limitations upon the state. But when the struggle between castes, classes and social groups is eliminated, when the unification of a people has been accomplished and there are no social groups oppressed by the state, then the people and the state are equivalent, and the state is finally deified. It is not absolutely necessary that the people should express their will in the form of a liberal democracy with a parliament ; it may be expressed in the form of an authoritarian democracy with a leader endowed with supreme power. Thus we may see that it is possible to have a leader with dictatorial powers and at the same time retain the old democracy. This is the case with Roosevelt : he is evoked by the need for radical social reforms, which always demand a strongly individual authority, initiative and responsibility.

In essence Mussolini says the same thing as Marx. Marx teaches that the conflict between personality and society existed only because of the conflict between classes. When class disappears, when the exploiting class, and hence class conflict, has been abolished, no conflict between personality and society will remain. For Mussolini the state is the absolute, for Marx it is society. But both maintain the same principle, both deny the tragic and eternal conflict between personality and the state or society, both deny the inalienable freedom of personality. The truth is just the reverse. The conflict of class and social groups has merely disguised the eternal conflict between personality and society, between personality and the state. And when there are no more classes, when society is socially democratized and unified, then there will be revealed in all its metaphysical depths the never-ending tragedy of the conflict between personality and society. In the same way, the moment the elementary problem of assuring the economic life of every human being is solved, there will at once appear the full sharpness of the problem of the spirit. This may be a problem for the perhaps distant future, but it now seems that human societies are destined to pass through the ordeals and temptations of ideocracy, of the absolute state, nation or society, the negation of spiritual liberty. Perhaps liberal democracy will not endure. Parliamentarianism with its regime of parties and the power of money is in decomposition. The old forms of democracy hinder the radical reform of human societies, and new forms are appearing, more mobile, more dynamic, more capable of swift action, better suited to the instincts of the mass of modern youth. Fascism is one of these evolving forms, arising out of the atmosphere of the world war and the world crisis which accompanied it.

The world evidently must pass through dictatorship which will in its turn vanish, once certain radical reforms of society are accomplished. Escape from dictatorship is possible only by moral rebirth and the application of creative spiritual forces. The old socialist parties are powerless—they have lost their enthusiasm, become bourgeois, they have been bureaucratized and are no longer capable of action. In this connection the fate of the German social-democrats is very revealing. We are entering a period of great difficulty for human personality, for freedom of the spirit, for higher culture. And the question poses itself: can these dictatorships confine themselves only to politics and economics, or is it inevitable that they also become dictatorships of world-view, of ideas, of the spirit, that is to say, the denial of all free spiritual life and work and conscience? In principle the first is possible, but what actually happens is the second, because of the decline in Christian faith. And we shall have spiritual war. It is already taking place in German Christianity, and it will spread over the whole world. We must battle against monism, for dualism, for the reality of the distinction between the spiritual and the natural-social, between the world of being and the objectivized world, between the Church and the State, between what is God's and what belongs to Cæsar.

It is surprising, as I noted above, that absolute monism, absolute ideocracy, is realizable without any real unity of belief.   Such a thing as unity of belief does not exist in a single society or state to-day.   An obligatory unity is attained by a sort of collective emotional demonic possession. Unity is attained by the dictatorship of a party which makes itself the equivalent of the state. From the sociological viewpoint it is very interesting that freedom is constantly diminishing in the world, not only in comparison with societies founded on liberal and democratic principles, but even in comparison with the old monarchical and aristocratic societies where, actually, there was more liberty, in spite of the fact that there was far greater unity in the matter of religious faith.   In the older social forms, really great liberty was assured for fairly limited groups — liberty was an aristocratic privilege.   When the circle was widened and society made uniform, instead of freedom being extended to all, it is non-freedom which becomes universal : all are equally subject to the state or to society.   A socially differentiated order preserved certain liberties for an elect group.   Freedom is an aristocratic rather than a democratic privilege.   Tocqueville saw in democracy a danger for liberty.   The same problem is posed by Marx and Mussolini as illustrated in Communism and Fascism.

The world has entered a period of the agony of the free spirit.   Man is shaken to his very foundations by the process of dehumanization. The ideal of man has been eclipsed. This is a trying period, but one of transition. It may be that man must be crucified and die, that he may rise again to new life. Neither Communism nor Fascism is that new life : they are only passing forms in which elements of truth are mingled with frightful untruth and injustice. These transition-forms are born of suffering and misfortune, not of creative abundance. All old authorities have collapsed, and the world is threatened with relapse into anarchy. The world has been stunned by the new forces which have entered it so unexpectedly. They entered the world at a time when the unity of faith had been lost, when scepticism had corroded and dissolved the old society. What are these new forces ?

CHAPTER III

NEW FORCES IN THE WORLD'S LIFE

I

NEW forces have entered world history. The process of democratization began a long time ago, but the end of the war witnessed the complete occupation of the stage of history by the mobilized masses. This is the basic factor of modern history. Before this, the masses had never been permitted to occupy the centre of the stage in any active role. But within history itself there was steadily growing up what I call the prosaicness of history : history has always based itself upon large numbers—upon the collective. States and social institutions were always created for the masses, for the average man and not for the spiritual aristocracy. Man has always been overwhelmed by large numbers ; the talented by the mass of the mediocre, quality by quantity. But the large number, the collective, never played so great a role as in our time. As I said above, the masses once lived and grew as do the plants, in organic structure and harmony, and their life was ordered by positive religious beliefs.

But the organic structure and harmony have decayed and religious beliefs have lost their power. And now at a moment in history so difficult that we are threatened with anarchy, the masses burst in upon the centre of the stage. But their entry is not altogether formless : they appear, organized into collectives. This entrance of the masses is accompanied by what amounts to an obsession for organization. Hence the tendency toward dictatorship, the search for a leader who will replace the fallen authorities.

Well-organized collectives, a striving toward unity in one huge collective—these are part of the new forces of our epoch. And the basis of these newly-formed collectives is usually organizations of youth, communist, fascist, nazi. Human society is evidently no longer able to live individualistically, but only in unions, fraternities, corporations, collectives. The divorced, individualistic, isolated life is a bourgeois result of capitalist society where man is a wolf to his fellows and every man thinks only of himself. This situation cannot continue. The bourgeois and individually profitable life was possible only for certain privileged people with a special calling, not for the average man nor the mass. The direct result of this new role of the mass, organized into collectives, and their participation in culture, is a lowering of cultural quality, a barbarization :

culture is now armed with the weapons of civilization.   The style of life is changing, as is the type
of popular interests and the direction of public
consciousness.   A quality-culture was connected
with aristocracy (not in the social sense, of course).
And this aristocratic element is now threatened
with extinction.   The cultural elite is under-
going a regular pogrom.   This is the case both
in Soviet Russia and in Hitlerist Germany.   That
Germany which once confessed a regular cult of
the intellectual, the professor, the philosopher,
the university, a cult which was often exaggerated
and almost comic, has now ceased completely to
respect these things and is ready to wipe them
off the slate.   The masses demand that men of
thought and cultural creativeness serve them,
fulfil " social " orders and commands.   Thinkers
are feeling the cruel results of the dictatorship of
dominant orthodoxy and dogmatics and are forced
to accept the prevailing symbolism.   In Italy
where the dictatorship of thought is comparatively
gentle, fascist youth not long ago destroyed the
library of the greatest living Italian philosopher,
Benedetto Croce, simply because he wished to
retain his liberty of thought and would not accept
the creed of Fascism.   These new dictatorships
demand a far sterner orthodoxy of men of
creative thought than ever was demanded in the
middle ages.   The forms taken by this demand for

orthodoxy in Russian Communism are well known.
Soviet Russia has become the classic instance of
" social orders " issued to cultural thinkers.

This means the end of individualism in the
worst sense. The egoist individualism of bourgeois culture should have been done away
with. In men of cultural creativeness the almost
vanished consciousness of the need for service
to something larger than the personal must be
aroused. But the process now at work in the
world means not only the end of individualism,
but also terrible danger to the eternal truth of
personalism, which means a threat to the very
existence of human personality. In the collective, personal consciousness is extinguished and
replaced by that of the collective itself. Thought
is regimented, and instead of personal conscience
we have the conscience of the group. The
change in consciousness is so radical that even
the attitudes toward truth and falsehood are
changed. What once was falsehood to the personal consciousness now becomes part of human
duty in the conscience of the collective. Think-
ing, as well as critical judgment, is compelled to
march in step.

Collectivism and the collective conscience are
not new in history. History began with it and
collectivism has always been present in history,
for the average man, for the mass. The herd

instinct has always been present in humanity, an evidence of its participation in the fallen state of the world. Personal originality in thought or conscience or creativity was always the rare inheritance of a few. The primitive clans with their totemistic cults lived under the sign of the collective, in them personality had not yet awakened, and the border between personality and the social group had not been recognized. Many of the taboos which fill the civilized epoch of history are inheritances from this primitive herd instinct, this primeval collective.

Throughout all his history man has lived in collectives, family, tribal, national, state or military; collectives of class or caste, of profession or of religion. And man has always thought and judged in tune with the consciousness of the collective to which he belonged. Thought was rarely personal; it was usually tribal or family thought. Thought has been on the basis of caste, the profession, the tribe. The average soldier thinks differently from the average civilian; the average Frenchman from the average German. The average noble or bourgeois thinks differently from the average peasant, the average doctor differently from the average lawyer. Personal originality rising above the family or class level has always been a rarity. It is a mistake to think that in the individualist epoch, in bourgeois society, thought and conscience were always personal : they were impersonal and average, adapting themselves to the prevailing type of man. The impersonal and inhuman power of money has determined the fate of man. The opinion of bourgeois society is a tyrant. It demands of man, of persons, quite impersonal judgments. Every atom must resemble every other. Instead of meaning personal originality and creativity, personal thought, individualism has usually meant egoism, profit, isolation, division, a wolf-like attitude toward one's neighbour, complete absence of the sense of super-personal service. Individualism has not been personalism at all; instead, it was another sort of tribal and collective instinct. Individualism is either a bourgeois attitude toward life, or the isolation of a few æsthetes. Personalism, on the other hand, is the realization in man of the image and likeness of God. In individualistic bourgeois society man has been socialized and objectivized, subject to the power of money and industrial development, his power of judgment has been subjected to bourgeois moral standards, but he has been constantly taught to think that he was serving society, the nation or the state. At the same time he remained " the economic man," an individualist in economic life, guided by individual, rather than social interests.

The collective of our epoch introduces a novelty. The collectives of former times consisted of various differentiated groups, national, family, professional or class. Now the collective is generalized and made universal. The world seems to be moving toward a universal collectivism in which all differentiation disappears. In Communism, Fascism or National-Socialism we see clearly this process of depersonalization: all must think alike, have the same opinions; all personal originality is lost in the collective.

This process of unification and universalization strikes hardest at the chosen individualist who belong to no group or collective. We are witnessing a reversion to the herd instinct, but in new, civilized and technicalized forms. The masses who have come into power want to live in these new, organized, but not organic, collectives. The mass-man is depersonalized, yet he can display more sacrifice and unselfishness than the bourgeois individualist. At the same time we see the influence of a factor which played a role as far back as the capitalistic society of the nineteenth century, and which served as the basis for the theories of Marx. This factor is economism.[1] The power of economics was never so strong as in our time. Now nothing can escape its influence. Everyone is troubled

[1] See next paragraph.

by worry : even those who feel secure for to-day are concerned about to-morrow. The life of the whole world moves beneath the sign of economism, and economic interests have put all things under their feet. With the masses living chiefly by economic interests, culture suffers fatally, since it becomes a needless luxury. By impoverishing all nations the world war has greatly strengthened the influence of economics. All governments are chiefly occupied with questions of finance and unemployment. The masses of mankind are concerned almost exclusively with earning their daily bread and even those who for the moment are rich and comfortable have lost all sense of stability and themselves await financial catastrophe. With appalling clarity it is revealed to us that the bases of the life of our fallen world are want and worry : the Biblical curse is realized, " in the sweat of thy brow shalt thou eat thy bread." The power of economic interests is bound up with over-population, which in Germany, for example, has become a fact which threatens the peace of Europe.

Capitalism gave birth to economism as a world-view, but it was itself born of economism. Economism is something more than the ascription of great significance to economic processes and development as conditions of human life

and culture : it is a perversion of the hierarchy
of values. The economism of the capitalist
world recognizes spirit as an epiphenomenon of
economics. And it is not Marx who is to blame
for this perversion. Marx discovered this idea
in the capitalist, bourgeois society of the nineteenth century and was so affected by it that
he considered it to be of universal significance.
But we are living in the decline of capitalism,
it has passed its period of flowering. The
capitalism of our day is a fallen capitalism which
is being remade into a new form of economics.
With financial capital at its head, capitalism is
no longer connected with liberalism or individualism. It is passing over from a liberal period
to one of state-control, since liberal, unregulated
capitalism has become patently dangerous for all
classes, even the bourgeoisie. In spite of Marx,
even the capitalists are dissatisfied with capitalism. This is especially evident in America, the
classic example of industrial capitalism. There
the necessity of some regulation of capitalism
is universally recognized as urgent, since unregulated capitalism has brought the country to
the verge of catastrophe.

The old form of capitalism no longer assures
the life of anyone. It can no longer feed man.
Whereas once the capitalist system exploited the
masses, now it puts them out on the street. It is

powerless to conquer unemployment. As has often been pointed out, there is no proper relation between production and demand. And this is a moral and metaphysical defect as well as purely economic, since it means that production does not exist for man, but man for production. This is why it is possible to destroy or dump into the sea huge quantities of grain, for purely economic interests, at a moment when millions are starving. Man is not the centre of economics : economic liberalism and individualism are at fault for not having placed him there. Capitalistic economy is deeply anti-personal : it dehumanizes economic life and makes man a thing. This is expressed in its present period of decline by the fact that it is becoming constantly more anonymous. Capitalism is itself breaking down the principle of private property : it is difficult to know who is a proprietor and just what he owns. The power of the banks is a faceless, anonymous power. The trusts are anonymous, impersonal institutions. It is even uncertain who is responsible for the misery under which the world is now suffering : there is no culprit, for he has no name. The unemployed do not know who is to blame for their bitter lot. Man is crushed by a vast shapeless, faceless and nameless power, money.

But the chief cosmic force which is now at

work to change the whole face of the earth and dehumanize and depersonalize man is not capitalism as an economic system, but technics, the wonder of our age. Man has become a slave to his own marvellous invention, the machine. We may well call our epoch the epoch of technics. Technics is man's latest and greatest love. At a time when he has ceased to believe in miracles, man still believes in the miracle of technics. Dehumanization is, first of all, the mechanization of human life, turning man into a machine. The power of the machine shatters the integrity of the human image. Economic life is seen to be completely separated from spiritual life, which is pushed further and further into the background and is no longer permitted to direct life in general. The machine was intended to liberate man from slavery to nature, to lighten his burden of labour, but instead of that it has enslaved man anew and cursed him with unemployment.

This proves that the whole of our social organism is afflicted with a terrible spiritual and moral disease, a truly bestial attitude of man to man. It is not enough to consider techicized capitalism as merely an economic category : it is a moral category as well, and directly related to man's attitude toward his fellows. As I pointed out in my pamphlet, *Man and the Machine*, technics have cosmic as well as social significance.

Technics have produced a new reality, something quite other than the reality of the natural, non-organic world. Beside the phenomena of organic and non-organic bodies there has appeared the organized body, formed not from the natural world, but from the world of history, from civilization. Modern technics indicate the end of the telluric period in the life of man. Man has ceased to be dependent on the earth, to feed himself from it. Technics mean a transition from organic, animal-and-vegetable life to organized life. The appearance of huge masses and collectives is one result of this condition. Man has ceased to live close to the earth, surrounded by animals and plants : he lives in a new metallic reality, breathes a new and poisoned air. The machine has a crushing effect on the human soul, it damages emotional life first of all, thus shattering the integrity of human personality. Even if a hard and virile nature can resist and overcome the power of the machine, the soul itself agonizes helplessly beneath its wheels.

Modern collectives are not organic but mechanical. The modern man can be organized only technically and the power of technics is in keeping with our democratic era. Technics rationalize human life, but this rationalization has irrational results, such as unemployment

which seems ever more clearly to be the future
in store for man. The social question is made
a matter above all of distribution, that is not
merely an economic, but a moral question. The
present state of the world calls for a moral and
spiritual revolution, revolution in the name of
personality, of man, of every single person.
This revolution should restore the hierarchy of
values, now quite shattered, and place the value
of human personality above the idols of production, technics, the state, the race or nationality, the collective. But now we must consider
one more of the modern forms of idol-making.

II

The age-old instincts of race and nationality
have suddenly burst forth in our world with
new force. National passion is tearing the world
and threatening the destruction of European
culture. This is one more proof of the strength of
atavism in human society, of how much stronger
than the conscious is the subconscious, of how
superficial has been the humanizing process of
past centuries. Where in the past the confirma-
tion and development of national individuality
meant humanization, modern Nationalism means
the dehumanization and bestialization of human
societies. It is a reversion from the category of
culture and history to that of zoology. It seems

as though the early conflict of tribe and race which preceded the formation of nationalities was being reborn as a cultural-historic form. We might be at the very beginning of the Middle Ages. The results of the Christian-humanistic process of unifying humanity seem to be disappearing. We are witnessing the paganization of Christian society. Nationalism is polytheism : it is incompatible with monotheism.

This process of paganization takes shocking forms in Germany, which wishes no longer to be a Christian nation, has exchanged the swastika for the cross and demands of Christians that they should renounce the very fundamentals of the Christian revelation and the Christian faith, and cast aside the moral teaching of the Gospels. France was long ago de-Christianized, but she was so thoroughly penetrated by humanism and enlightenment that she has been prevented from becoming a pagan nation. In Germany, where humanistic enlightenment was always weak, a religion of pagan particularism is attempting to overthrow Christian universalism. The spiritual-personal concept of man is being replaced by the naturalist and zoological, and the same methods are employed for the regulation of human life as those employed in stock-breeding. The methods proposed for the development and preservation of a pure German race are very similar to those in use for the same purpose with dogs and horses. German racialism is a romantic naturalism and it contains elements of the reaction of "nature," of blood, of the earth and the spirit of the people, that is telluric forces against the power of technics. But it uses the methods of modern technics and apes the approach of the Soviets. Sterilization, eugenics, the prohibition of mixed marriages, state interference with personal life— all these are far from being developments of natural life. This is a most completely planned and dehumanized technical civilization. Purely zoological instincts, romantically idealized and transformed into a naturalist mysticism are equipped with modern civilized technique.

This new emergence of nationalism and racialism is paradoxical because we live in an epoch so universalist that it greatly resembles the Hellenistic age. Everything has planetary significance. And against this background of basic universalism the particularism of modern racial and national movements stands out sharply. Such things as completely closed, isolated, autarchic groups no longer exist : everything goes on under the eyes of the whole world. Modern technics have a universalizing and unifying character ; they remain the same in any form of Nationalism. There is no such thing as organic originality. Thus the nationalism of Eastern peoples is merely the imitation of Europe and its armed technics. Even the sport and technics which interest so many groups of nationalist youth to-day are of a thoroughly international order.

Throughout history we can trace two tendencies, that toward individualization and that toward universalization. Both are not only inevitable, but justified, in cosmic life. But their harmonic adjustment has almost never been attained, one or the other has always held undue predominance. Just like everything else in the history of our fallen world, the proper harmonization of the individualizing with the universalizing force has never succeeded ; like everything else, they have been distorted by sinful desire and idolatry. Nationalism and internationalism have equally impaired the integrity of humanity. Both the Nationalism and the etatism of our time are forms of idolatry. The Christian truth that there is no longer Greek nor Jew, which was of course, no denial of the fact of national individuality, is violently overthrown and the peoples of Europe are reverting to the old, pagan ideas of nationality. The unity of mankind, toward which, in principle, at least, the processes of both Christianization and humanization were leading us are now denied in principle and in intent, and human unity is threatened with dissolution.   This is a proof that the natural unification of humanity is unattainable : such unity can be attained only spiritually.   The unity of mankind is " God-in-manity."

Nationalism turns nationality into a supreme and absolute value to which all life is subordinated.   This is idolatry.   The nation replaces God. Thus Nationalism cannot but come into conflict with Christian universalism, with the Christian revelation that there is neither Greek nor Jew, and that every man has absolute value.   Nationalism uses everything as its own instrument, as an instrument of national power and prosperity.   For Nationalism, religion and the church are purely national-historic categories.   A Russian should be Orthodox not because that is the true faith, but because orthodoxy has been an historic-national force, it participated in the development of the Russian state and Russian culture.   In the same way a Pole should be Catholic, a German Lutheran, an Englishman Anglican, just as a Turk should be Mohammedan.   Nationalism leads directly to polytheism, to pagan particularism.   During the war we saw how the German God, the Russian God, the French and English Gods were at war with each other. Nationalism cannot accept universal religious truth : in its consciousness religion remains at the pre-Christian level, the stage of Judaism,

the religion of a tribal god who has not yet
become a universal deity. Or it is like paganism
before the development of the philosophic idea
of one God. Nationalism was foreign to the
ideas of the Christian universalism of the Middle
Ages : it is a product of modern history which
has lost its sense of unity and is moving toward
particularism.

French Nationalism, for example, derives from
the French Revolution, from the idea of the
supremacy of the nation. The older aristocratic
and monarchical France did not know nationalism
in the sense in which it has arisen in the nineteenth and twentieth centuries. It must be
admitted that Nationalism, as one of the degrees
of the individualization of being, has undoubted
and positive value. Culture always had national
character and roots. An international culture is
impossible. Only technics are truly international
and they have a strong internationalizing influence.
Nationalism is a cultural and historic fact. It is
an attitude toward facts, but it transforms a
natural fact into an idol. Nationalism has no
Christian roots and it is always in conflict with
Christianity.

But Christianity is certainly not cosmopolitanism, which is a unification of being, a denial of
the individual degrees of being and the confirma-
tion of abstract, in the place of concrete unity.

Cosmopolitanism is general rather than universal.
The universal is something concretely one : it
does not depend upon numbers.   Christianity is
ecumenism and concrete unity, taking into itself
all transformed and enlightened individual being.
Nationalism is above all an emotional phenomenon
and in a dispute with Nationalism all intellectual
arguments are powerless.

There is an anecdote which, whether the event
really took place or not, has true philosophic
meaning.   In a French salon, where there were
gathered a number of prominent political personalities, one Frenchman expressed his disgust at
the English who always consider themselves the
first nation in the world, with a supreme world-
mission, and refuse to recognize that other nations
might be their equals.   Another replied : " Why
does this disturb you about the English : the
French think the same of themselves."   " Well,"
was the reply, " but with us it is true."   All
national disputes close with the same anecdote.
This is because the attitude toward one's nation
is erotic, an attitude of erotic choice.   Our nation,
our country is as dear to us as the face of a
beloved woman.   But Nationalism sets eros over
against ethos, and transforms the natural erotic
in its attitude into a supreme principle or doctrine.
In principle it affirms only the erotic and denies
the ethical.   Hence its inevitable conflict, not

only with Christianity, but with general humanistic morals. The purely erotic relationship
excluding the ethical, cannot be maintained
toward anything on earth; not toward the nation,
not toward humanity. We must have not only
eros, but ethos, connected with the dignity of
personality.

Nationalism denies this. Nationalism involves
not only love of one's own, but hatred of other
nations, and hatred is usually a stronger motive
than love. Nationalism preaches either seclusion,
isolation, blindness to other nations and culture,
self-satisfaction and particularism, or else expan-
sion at the expense of others, conquest, subjection,
imperialism. And in both cases it denies Christian conscience, contraverts the principle and the
habits of the brotherhood of man. Nationalism is
in complete contradiction to a personal ethic; it
denies the supreme value of human personality.
Modern Nationalism dehumanizes ethics, it demands of man that he renounce humanity. It is
all one and the same process, in Communism as in
Nationalism. Man's inner world is completely at
the mercy of collectivism, national or social.

Nationalism and Socialism (in its broad sense)
are two forces in our modern world which fight
against each other, but on occasion can marvel-
lously adapt themselves to one another and
even be mingled together. In its more classical,

Marxist form, Socialism is hostile not merely to Nationalism, but to the national; it is bound up with cosmopolitanism. This is the point on which the national and the social most often come to blows. Marx proclaimed the principle that the labourer has no fatherland: "Workers of the world unite!" The classes which are cruelly exploited and suppressed by their fellow-countrymen cannot feel much national solidarity and brotherhood with them. For the exploited of one country, the exploited and oppressed of another are nearer than the exploiters of their own. Social- and class-solidarity is contrasted with that within a nation. Men unite and separate on a vertical, instead of a horizontal plane. Marx has been criticized for having destroyed the reality of fatherland, for the denial of all patriotic and national feeling. But it would be more just to say that Marx merely recognized an existing situation. It was capitalism and its crying social injustice which destroyed all national feeling in the working classes. The internationalism of the workers is just as comprehensible and easily explained, just as justified emotionally, as is their atheism. Patriotism and Nationalism have been too often used to conceal the interests of the ruling classes, just as have been religion and the church. But this does not solve either problem: that of nationality or that of religion.

Marx failed to realize the depth of both and of course he underestimated the significance of national instincts, as was proved by the reaction of socialist workers at the beginning of the war.

Cosmopolitanism is really the logical product of the capitalist world and technical civilization, which separate man from the telluric, natural bases of his life. The armament-makers, producing poison gas for war, usually hide behind Nationalism and patriotism, demanding war to a victory, but in reality they are cosmopolitans. Socialist-internationalists are right both when they claim to be international and when they claim to be national : where the social and the national conflict, justice is more often on the side of the social. This is usually a conflict between ethos and eros, although an erotic attitude toward social justice is also possible. One may love his own country and his own people, but demand a worthy human existence and the realization of justice in their life.

The social re-birth of Nationalism is characteristic of our time. It has ceased to be the heritage of the ruling bourgeois classes and becomes that of the popular mass. Modern Nationalism is popular and democratic. In the social sphere, its partisans are chiefly in the petit-bourgeois, the de-classed and proletarianized elements of society, together with the peasant masses, close to the soil. On the face of it, one would think that the whole of a given people stood behind their Nationalism, and that progress toward the social democratization of Nationalism is undeniable. This makes possible such a development as German National-Socialism which combines elements of both Nationalism and Socialism. As a matter of fact the socialist elements are pretty thoroughly overshadowed by those of nation and race. Still the really popular character of Naziism can be as little denied as that of Fascism.

The international position of Germany is responsible for the union between the social element, connected with the proletarianization of considerable groups of the German people and an aggressive national element. The German people felt themselves disgraced and knew a sense of solidarity in humiliation. After the war Germany was forced into the position of the proletariat among the nations and this produced National-Socialism. But the Hitler brand of Socialism is still largely demagogic. The widely-proclaimed national revolution has not yet arrived at the reform of society. Even Roosevelt is accomplishing more radical social reforms. Both emotions, national and social, have become the chief instruments of demagogy. The masses are led by the most shameless demagogic methods. Even Socialism in our day has taken on this

character and lost the idealism it had in the last
century.   But modern Nationalism is still more
demagogical : it bears the unmistakable imprint
of spiritual plebeianism.   For that matter, so
does our epoch, itself.   Nationalism takes unto
itself the symbolism of race, and it is possible to
have a popular revolutionary movement under
this flag, instead of that of class.   What is
racialism ?

In Germany racialism has taken the form of a
collective religious insanity.   The revolution in
Germany took place under the sign of nation and
race, just as in Russia under that of social class.
But it is unwise to take such symbolism too
seriously in the case of mass movements.   The
symbolism is a relative factor, and processes
which are very similar may adopt quite different
symbols.   Mass movements always demand a
unifying and strength-giving symbol, which
always becomes the test of orthodoxy.   All who
do not accept the symbol are accursed and cast
out as heretics.   And in our day the categories
of heresy and orthodoxy have become very
important social factors.   It may be noted in
passing that orthodoxy has always been a social
phenomenon, always determined by the social
collective.   Heresy is departure from the conscience of the social collective, and in our day
the distinction between orthodoxy and heresy, as

evidenced in the domination of the mass over personal conscience, has again become a decisive factor in politics.   This is clearly a reversion to the Middle Ages.   In Russia for the past eighteen years there has reigned the tyrannous orthodoxy of Marxism, albeit a Marxism which is quite untrue to Marx.   And human life is deliberately crippled, in the name of that orthodoxy.

In Germany there has developed the orthodoxy of racialism.   This orthodoxy has a much more difficult position, since it is not backed by such a well-developed theory as Marxism, but it too, cripples human life, and with its forced sterilization for the sake of the purity of the race, even goes farther than Communism.   Is there any scientific or philosophic foundation for racialism? Racialism is rather mythological than scientific, but mass movements are always inspired by mythology, rather than science.   Even our epoch, so proud of its science and its technical achievement is steeped in myth : science and technics have themselves become myths.   German Nationalism always had in it more of racialism than that of other peoples.   French Nationalism, for example, has no connection with racialism.   But in Germany, neither racialism nor anti-Semitism is surprising : they are old diseases of the German spirit, bearing witness to the fact that Christianity never really succeeded in changing the depths of

German paganism.   The idea of German imperialism, the consciousness of a great German mission
and the sense of German pride, runs through all
German thought of the nineteenth century.   Most
of German philosophy and science is imbued with
it.   Fichte was the herald of the militant idea of a
German mission in the world.   But since he was
also a humanist and a devoted admirer of the
French Revolution, he considered the Germans
first of all as men and saw in German culture the
foremost if not the exclusive bearer of humanity.
Fichte was also an anti-Semite and refused to
accord to Jews the ordinary rights of man.
This appears clearly in his article on the
French Revolution, written, to be sure, in his
revolutionary period.

The philosophy of Hegel provided the real
basis for the idea of the special mission of the
German people.   Hegel saw in the Prussian state
the incarnation of the world-spirit.   This same
emotional expression of German Nationalism may
be found in most of the romanticists.   Hitler, for
instance, finds his inspiration in Wagner.   The
whole of Wagner's work is an expression of
militant and aggressive German messianism.   He
was a true anti-Semite and racialist : one of
the founders of the racialist anti-Semite ideology.
Nietzsche stands quite apart from this.   In some
respects he serves as inspiration for German

imperialism, for the German cult of might.
Much that is similar may be found in Marx,
especially his attitude toward Russia and the
Slav, or toward anti-Semitism. Düring, who is
a sort of anarchist, was an extreme anti-Semite,
as were Langben, the author of a book on
Rembrandt, Chamberlain and Woltmann. All
these made attempts more or less successful to
provide scientific basis for the racialist theory,
the myth of a chosen Aryan race which was, of
course, the Germans.

The real founder of the race theory, however,
was the French Gobineau, a keen thinker and
writer of the aristocratic type, quite disdainful
of coarse anti-Semitism, just as of anything
coarse and unrefined. He is the creator of the
myth of the chosen Aryan race and the noble
mission of the Germans, whom, by the way,
he held to have become an impure race. For
Gobineau, the theory of the inequality of different
races served above all as the basis for the aristocratic idea, the justification of aristocratic culture.
In contrast to the modern German racialists,
Gobineau was a pessimist and believed in the
inevitable decline of races and cultures. In
France, Gobineau had small success and his race
theory was not accepted. But it took root in
Germany and developed a much coarser form
than its original. Chamberlain was also a very

cultured thinker, although nothing is more pitiful and even comic than his attempt to prove that Jesus Christ was not a Jew. The coarsening process has continued, until in our day what began as an aristocratic theory has become thoroughly plebeian and serves to inspire the masses.

Modern science considers the race theory pure mythology, and refuses to take seriously the idea of the " Aryan " race. There is no such thing as a pure race, not to mention the German nation, which is the result of complex mixtures.· The only race, perhaps, which approaches racial purity is the Hebrew. The very concept of race is indistinct and is often based upon confounding elements belonging to zoology with those which pertain to human history. Race is a zoological category, and in this it differs from nationality which is a cultural-historic category. The most terrible thing in racialism is that it is a rude materialism which has taken a mystical character. Racialism makes the spirit dependent upon shape of skull and colour of hair. This is absolute naturalist determinism, hostile to spirit and the spiritual, since the spirit is above all, liberty.

Racialism is a ruder form of materialism than economic materialism itself, since the social really belongs more to the psychic realm and less to the material, than does the biological or the zoological. According to the racialist theory, man is an animal, biologically determined by his blood and his anatomical structure. The theory affirms the fatality of inheritance. But it is impossible, anywhere in history, to find a real race in the accepted zoologic-naturalist sense of the word : a real race existed only in prehistoric times. In history we have only nationality, something which is the result of complex cultural and historical processes. It is not because of their blood that the French are called a Latin race, since there is very little real Latin blood in their veins and they are actually a complex racial mixture which contains among others, a strong Celtic element. The French are called Latin because they accepted Latin culture and formed themselves in it. There is no such thing as a Latin race. It is more than doubtful whether the Russians are a Slavic race, there is too strong an admixture of Finnish, Tartar, and in the upper layers of society, especially since Peter the Great, of German blood. Russians are Scythians : they are probably less Slavic than the Poles or the Czechs. Prussia is an ancient Slavic land and there is much Slavic blood in the present-day Prussians.

What, then, is the real significance of a racialism which takes forms so terrible (from the

Christian point of view) as that now rampant
in Germany ? Racialism is a purely Hebrew
ideology. The only classic example in history
of the racialist ideal is that afforded by the Jews.
It was the Jewish race which strove for racial
purity, opposed mixed marriages and all sorts
of mingling with others, strove to remain a
world closed to outsiders. Judaism gave religious significance to blood-relationship and
bound up inseparably the religious element with
that of Nationalism. The Messianic consciousness of any people is always an evidence of the
Jewish spirit. Exclusiveness, the loyalty to one's
own things and people only, is one of the prime
qualities of Judaism. Thus the anti-Semite may
well be accused of Jewish practice and spirit.
It is just we non-Jews who should be far from
all racialism, exclusive Nationalism, all Messianism. Such " Aryan " groups as the Hindus or
the Greeks are more naturally individualists, in
the ancient, rather than the modern meaning
of that word. They set more value upon soul,
spirit, bodily form, than upon the fate of the
national collective. Fanaticism, intolerance or
exclusiveness are not characteristic traits of these
groups.

Even if, in the world of Judaism, there is
some justification for racialism, it has no basis
at all in Christianity. The mere consideration

of the " Aryan paragraph " is unworthy of a
Christian, although it is now demanded of
Christians in Germany.   Racialist anti-Semitism
inevitably leads to anti-Christianity, as we see in
Germany to-day.   That Germano-Aryan Christianity now being promoted is a denial of the
Gospels and of Christ Himself.   The ancient religious conflict between Christianity and Judaism,
a real conflict by the way, has taken such a turn
in our difficult and uncertain times, that militant anti-Judaism turns out to be anti-Christianity.
Truly Christian anti-Judaism is directed, not
against the Bible or the Old Testament, but
against the Talmudic-rabbinic Judaism which
developed after the Jews' refusal to accept Christ.
But when religious anti-Judaism becomes racialist anti-Semitism, it inevitably turns into anti-
Christianity, for the human origins of Christianity
are Hebrew.   It is proper for orthodox Jews
to be racialists : they may be at enmity with
" Aryan " Christians.   But it is impossible, it is
forbidden, for a true Christian to be a racialist
and to hate the Jews.   This is one of the
advantages of Christianity.

From the Christian or the purely humane
viewpoint, the race theory is much worse than
the class theory.   It carries dehumanization much
deeper than the idea of class.   According to the
Marxist theory a man of the moribund bourgeois

class still has hopes of salvation by changing his class-consciousness; he always has the possibility of adopting the Marxist theory and becoming a communist or even a peoples' commissar. According to the race theory there is no hope of salvation, whatever: if you were born a Jew or a negro, no change of consciousness or belief or conviction can save you, you are doomed. A Jew may become a Christian: that does him no good. Even if he becomes a national-socialist, he cannot be saved. It is just as impossible to become a true German " Aryan " as to become a Jew. Both are born, not made. This is absolute determinism, fatalism. But Christianity is a religion of spiritual liberty: it denies fatalism or determinism. And since the fatalism of race is more fundamental than that of class, the former involves the greater dehumanization. From the Christian point of view, Hitlerism is more dangerous than Communism, since the latter struggles openly and directly against Christianity as against all religion, while Hitlerism demands a violent deformation of Christianity from within, altering the Christian faith itself in favour of the racialist theory and the dictatorship of the Third Reich.

Both Nationalism and racialism are inevitably connected with etatism. The realization of some great mission by a race or a nation, the accomplishment of its imperialistic will, demands power and authority. Since Nationalism can be realized only in the state, it strives to take the state into its own hands. Without capturing the state, Nationalism remains merely an emotional condition. Modern Nationalism has more connection with the state than with culture. In fact modern Nationalism lays small store by culture, often even turning away from the national cultural tradition. Hitlerism is especially untrue to the best traditions of German culture; it is not at all interested in having the German people remain a nation of philosophers and poets. But free science and deep respect for learning is the tradition of German culture, now completely rejected by the German Nationalism of to-day. To-day's Nationalism is inspired not by the will to truth, but by the will to power. "Down with truth, down with justice, if only we can be powerful!" seems to be modern Germany's slogan. This attitude needs a powerful state for its instrument.

The same was true of the old Russian Nationalism. It was never interested in Russian culture, but only in the might of the state. Its heroes were generals, ministers and governors, rather than poets, artists, philosophers, scientists, reformers or prophets. The Nationalism of postwar Russia exhibits the same traits: there is the same will to power, the same preference of the state over culture. Without etatism, without control of the power of the state as its instrument, without an absolute state, Nationalism cannot flourish. The power of the state is objectivized Nationalism. True, creative, national culture cannot admit intention in its formation. It is impossible consciously to set about making a national art or philosophy : one must love the truth, love justice and beauty. Philosophy may have a certain national character in the problems dealt with, but it will not exist at all unless it seeks truth above all else. The national quality of a culture is an unconscious, organic process, never arrived at by intention or premeditation. The politics of a state, on the other hand, may be intentionally and deliberately national, or better, nationalistic. It has yet to be demonstrated that Nationalism in the form of a dictatorship, pro-duces anything creative in the cultural realm : dictators seem usually to have no time for culture. But in the life of the state, a dictatorship can accomplish much : this is the sole productive sphere for active national will. Even where the state is considered to be not an end in itself, but an instrument of the race, Nationalism is inevitably not only the pagan worship of nation-ality, but also the pagan worship of the state, etatism. Modern Nationalism is connected with

the idea of a totalitarian state, and both Nationalism and etatism are based upon an anti-personal
ethic.   Organized masses want to live in absolute
states and seem not to value personal life, in-
dependent of the state.   They are not interested
in cultural creativeness, the product of spiritual
freedom.   In the last analysis, all despotism is a
transformed primitive Communism.

III

The world is entering an epoch of Cæsarism ;
and this Cæsarism, like all others, will be plebeian
in character.   It represents a plebeian uprising
against the aristocratic element in culture.   The
modern " leader," perhaps the predecessor of
the coming Cæsar, is a leader of the masses.   He
is the psychological product of the modern collective.   And he leads the masses by demagogy.
Once this fails him as an instrument, he loses his
power and is overthrown.   The "leader" depends
entirely upon the masses, which he rules despotic-
ally : he depends altogether on the psychology
of the collective, its emotions and instincts.
His authority is based altogether upon the
subconscious.

The subconscious always plays a large part in
the process of governing.   But it is surprising
to note how authority in our modern world,
based upon the subconscious and irrational,

adopts the methods of extreme rationalism, the technicalization of human life : it proclaims rationalized state planning, not only for economics, but for human thought and conscience, even for personal sexual and erotic life. Modern rationalization and technicalization are controlled by subconscious and irrational instincts, the instincts of violence and domination. This is true of both Germany and Soviet Russia. Of course modern etatism, the pretence of the kingdom of Cæsar to absolute significance, is diametrically opposed to Christianity. This may be the central meaning of the events of our time. The absolute ideocratic, totalitarian state comes inevitably into conflict with freedom of religious conscience, denies the Christian's right to liberty in his own spiritual life. The state would become the church. The distinction between the things of Cæsar and the things of God is constantly being erased in our fallen world, and this always indicates that the Kingdom of Cæsar is attempting to swallow up the Kingdom of God. This is revealed with unusual clarity in modern Germany.

In our fallen world, conflict is inevitable between the things of Cæsar and the things of God. The denial of the dualism of spirit and nature, freedom and necessity, the individual and society, is the source of despotism and

tyranny.   The complete elimination of that dualism would mean the transfiguration of the world,
a new heaven and a new earth.   But the kingdom of Cæsar, in various metamorphoses, attempts
to eliminate this dualism in a demoniac and
tyrannous manner.   Nationalism is one of the
roads toward tyranny of the things of Cæsar over
the spirit.   Only progress in the direction of
lessening the sovereignty of national states and
toward a world-federation of peoples will save
us from this tyranny.   Cultures should remain
national, rather than states.   This is exactly the
reverse of the claims of modern Nationalism.   But
one fears that the world will attain such an order
only after a considerable portion of humanity
has been wiped out.   We live under the sign
of bloodthirstiness and murder in tyrannous
states.   Modern economics, technics, Communism, Nationalism and racialism are all possessed
with the blood lust, and nourished by hatred.

And finally one more force must be noted
which has now entered history and threatens the
stability of European culture.   The peoples of
the East, the " coloured " races, now wish to take
an active part in history ; to be subjects instead
of objects.   The end of Europe's monopoly of
culture is approaching.   The reaction of East upon
West, which, it would seem, had been discontinued
since the Renaissance, is renewed.   Along with

the bursting forth of militant Nationalism we see
the universalization of mankind. The awakening
of the eastern nations, hitherto considered solely
as colonies, is a hard blow at Europe, first of all
in the economic sphere. But the colonies have
ceased to be the willing objects of capitalistic exploitation. The attitude of the Christian nations
of the West toward the non-Christian nations of
the East has been anything but Christian. The
resultant unpleasant associations have seriously
compromised Christianity in the whole world.
A few missionaries have demonstrated true
heroism and sanctity, but in general it has not
been a Christian face or attitude which the West
has shown toward the races of the East. And we
now have to pay for that mistake. Europe, in
so far as she remains Christian, must adopt a
Christian attitude toward the East, not that of the
exploiter. The white race can no longer play
the role of a superior civilizing agent to the
coloured races. The peoples of the East, Japanese,
Chinese, Indians have begun to adopt Western
civilization ; they have become materialists, have
learned Nationalism from the West. And only in
a very small measure have they accepted the light
of Christian truth. The old religions of the East
are decaying. Even the Hindu, more spiritual
by far than the bourgeois and materialist West,
is losing his spirituality and becoming civilized.

Thus great human masses, vastly outnumbering those of Europe, have actively entered history, and entered at the moment when they have acquired the worst phases of European civilization.   All this makes the world-crisis all the more acute and opens really frightful perspectives to our vision.   We have entered a period of decadence and anarchy, and at the same time men were never so possessed by the idea of organization, planning, compulsory unity, state absolutism, as now.   The roots of all this must be sought in the plane of the spiritual, in the crisis of Christianity and of religious consciousness in general, in the decline of spirituality.   And only a new spirituality, which has not yet defined itself as an historical force, can bring real recovery.

CHAPTER IV

CULTURE AND CHRISTIANITY

I

EVERYONE talks, nowadays, of the crisis of culture, and much fear is expressed for its future. This has become a general opinion. The crisis in culture is sociologically due to the fact that there is an aristocratic, qualitative element in every high culture, which is gravely endangered by any process of democratization and levelling-down, by the domination of the mass. We live in an epoch of plebeian revolt against every aristocratic element in culture. In so far as culture is concerned, the new authoritarian states are truly plebeian in character, and really signify the dominance of quantity over quality. Græco-Roman culture was aristocratic in principle, a culture based upon the support and protection of quality. The culture of the Renaissance was aristocratic as well. It developed because of leisure, the possibility of expressing creative plenitude, it presupposed inequality. Culture never existed for the whole mass of mankind, never could be a satisfaction of all its needs and

desires. A national culture has never meant
that it existed at the level, and carried out the
orders, of the popular mass ; rather, it meant
that a given culture was the expression of the
spirit of the nation. Hence genius could express
true national culture better than the mass. But
at the present time it is increasingly demanded of
culture that it be national in the sense of corres-
ponding to the needs and desires of the masses.
This changes culture into something so different
as to need a new name. Sometimes this new
phenomenon is called civilization, but this is a
purely conditional terminology.

The domination of the mass and the impersonal
collective, which at one place takes the form of
a bourgeois democracy with the dictatorship of
money although always disguised and secret, and
at another the form of the authoritarian state with
the openly avowed dictatorship of leaders—this
creates a most difficult situation for creative
cultural forces, for a cultural elite. This cultural
elite seems to be in its death agony : its situation
both moral and material is becoming ever more
unbearable. In a liberal democracy the cultural
elite depends on capital and the vulgar tastes of
the crowd ; in an authoritarian or a communist
democracy it depends upon the dictated world-
view, an authority which pretends to organize
the spirit. We live in an epoch of " dictated

social order." The mass determines what shall be the accepted culture, art, literature, philosophy, science, even religion. And there is no social demand for culture of a higher order, for spiritual culture, for real art or real philosophy. The social demand now is chiefly for technics, for applied natural science, for economics. There is no desire for the things of the spirit. Spiritual energy is switched over to be applied to objects of anything but the spiritual order. The intellectuals are socially defenceless; their existence is deprived of all material support. They are all too often compelled to feel their uselessness, and to adapt themselves to the new conditions in order to escape complete catastrophe.

The situation of the initiators and creators of spiritual culture has never been easy. This was true even in the epoch of the Renaissance. Time and again they created, without knowing for whom their work was intended, but their creativity was comparatively free. Materially, the writers, scientists, artists and musicians of that era were dependent upon their patrons, but they lived in a complex society, differentiated rather than made uniform as is the tendency to-day; they were under no dictatorship of the spirit and could sail on any tack they chose. The capitalism of the nineteenth century with its secret dictatorship of money, deformed and

tarnished the purity of culture, adapted it to
the interests of the bourgeois classes. In principle, the creative minds in culture were given
complete liberty, but actually they suffered
material pressure, loneliness, poverty and lack
of comprehension. Many of the creators of
culture of the liberal, bourgeois epoch, longed
for a "popular" or an "organic" culture. But
social isolation is a characteristic phenomenon
for the culturally creative minds in a bourgeois
epoch. There have been times when thinkers
were proud of their isolation and strove to
remain within it. Sometimes it was a group
that was isolated, a remote and lonely elite.
Ancient Greek culture was religious, truly popular, "organic." But this was quite another sort
of popularity from that of our democratic day,
since the masses were part of a religiously
sanctified hierarchic organism. There was no
great gap between the intellectual class and
popular life. This was a "socially-dictated"
culture in the good sense of the word, an
order which permitted and even postulated an
aristocratic, qualitative basis for culture. The
individualism of the Renaissance and bourgeois epochs is foreign to the Greek type of
culture.

The culture of ancient Greece was a culture
"socially dictated" to a greater extent than is

usually thought : art was not at all " pure," it played a role of service to society. Greek culture was at once popular and aristocratic. This combination of popularity and organic quality in culture is characteristic of earlier " organic " epochs. In our day, with its tendencies to collectivism, that is all changed. The masses participate in culture. This is both right and necessary : the masses must not remain in darkness. In the past the masses participated in culture by way of religion, and the culture of the broad masses was almost exclusively a religious culture. Religion was the meeting-place of the masses with the aristocratic cultural class. Only religion is capable of making such a combination : neither philosophy nor science, nor enlightenment, neither art nor literature can do this. Deprived of religious basis, any high-qualitative culture inevitably becomes separated from popular life and an isolated cultural elite is produced, which keenly feels its uselessness to the people.

Humanist culture was never popular : it was the culture of an upper, intellectual class which had no real social foundation. The thoroughly justified process of democratizing culture, of communicating it to the popular mass, has the natural reaction of lowering the qualitative level. This process means that two things are happening : the cultural level of the masses is raised, their cultural interest is aroused, but at the same time the masses begin to dominate culture and adapt it to their own level.   The culture of an elite is left isolated, becomes refined to the point where it exhibits signs of fatal illness and its representatives acquire a taste for death.   This is cultural decadence, a misuse of the sources of life.   Another part of the culturally creative try to save themselves by adapting themselves to the masses, to their tastes and demands, by trying to live up (or down) to the people's will.   And the very existence of a cultural elite, divorced from the life of the people, becomes more and more useless and abnormal.   Such a group has no future.   This crisis of qualitative culture, this sad fate of the intellectuals, is a situation evidently inescapable save by a spiritual revolution in the world, a religious renaissance.   Such a cultural renaissance is impossible because the world has grown too old.   Only a religious renaissance is possible.   This alone is capable of solving the problem of the right relationship between the aristocratic and the democratic, the personal and the social elements in culture.

Russian Communism and German National-Socialism are dictated world-views, dictatorship over the spirit.   Hence both are cultures created " by order."   In both countries this has taken abnormal forms which smother true cultural creativeness. Thus there is realized the ideal of collective, truly national culture of which some of the thinkers at the end of the nineteenth century and the beginning of the twentieth dreamed, Richard Wagner in Germany, and in Russia, V. Ivanoff and the symbolists. Thus culture is cleansed of individualism.

The end of the Renaissance is approaching, as I have said so many times. Is there any truth or justification in this process? Can its results be justly compared with the old liberalism and individualism? I believe there is much good in the new, and that the old liberalism and individualism are outworn and decadent. It is right to consider cultural creativeness as the service of a super-personal ideal. The egoism of an intellectual class cannot be justified, and the idea of service has almost disappeared in the renaissance-liberal era. But the idea of serving a super-personal purpose is not opposed to freedom of the spirit, to creative liberty. On the contrary, it is realizable only by means of this freedom. Creative service is voluntary: it cannot be put into a compulsory service like the army. A dictatorship over the spirit abolishes creative liberty and corrupts the culturally creative. It demands treason to their ideals, inclines them to servility and under threat of the knout it demands their fulfilment of the orders of the mass. A dictated world-view paralyses creative conscience and the only thing which can stand against it is the heroic resistance of free conscience.

The bribery of these creators of culture has been made easy because their situation, both spiritually and materially, is so difficult. Without social protection, they have become the typical unemployed. The intellectual class is threatened either with disappearance for lack of use or with becoming obedient servants to the ideocratic state, with its dictatorship over the spirit. The upper intellectual class has long been living a closed and isolated life, deprived of any broad social basis, and apart from the common life of the people. We have seen a complete separation between the theoretical and the practical mind, between intellect and action, between the spirit and the material. This has produced debility and decadence.

Humanism, that foundation of European culture, was unable to restore unity and to support the cultured class, once cosmic winds began to blow. Humanism is unable to resist the process of technicizing life, the rise of the masses to power, the process of democratization. It cannot save the aristocratic element in culture, or personal originality. Now an attempt is being made to restore unity by rough dictatorship, based upon dehumanization. The ideas of the nineteenth and twentieth centuries about "organic" culture and the organic social order are romantic ideas, and they have suffered irreparable damage under the blows of an ever-more-powerful technics. The world seems to be moving not toward an organic, vital unity, but to an organized and technical unity. And when in the modern cosmic and social unrest the question of man himself is raised, of man's salvation from the dehumanization of all life, we come inescapably to the question of religion, to the present spiritual crisis and the appearance in the world of a new spirituality.

II

We are witnessing a judgment not on history alone, but upon Christianity in history, upon Christian humanity. Christianity in history has been not only the revelation of God, but also a work of man. And this work of man has been both good and bad. The purity of revelation has often been sullied by the human element, the human consciousness through which it has been filtered. The sins of Christians in history are great and numerous. How many have been the false theophanies man has imagined! Too often the human has been passed off for the

divine. The history of Christianity, of the
Church, is a divine-human process, and in it, as
in every life-process, there have been pathological
elements, elements of decadence. The postulate
of free will offers the possibility for the failure
of Christianity in history. Christianity is not
God, not Christ Himself, although God and
Christ are active in Christianity. Christianity is
human history, and in it are represented all the
contradictions of human existence.

Christianity, Christian humanity, has passed
through all sorts of the temptations of this world,
often disguised as holy things. A decadent
freedom, presenting itself as the true will of God,
has been at work in Christian history. The
judgment on Christianity is a judgment upon the
false theophanies, the false sanctification of the
natural and the historical. Too much of the
merely relative and unworthy has been declared
sacrosanct. The processes of sanctifying the
natural-historical, processes really social in their
origin, have gained final predominance over those
forces working for the transfiguration of life,
over the prophetic element in religion. And the
judgment on Christianity in history is always a
prophetic judgment: it demands an outbreaking
of the prophetic spirit directed toward the transfiguration, and not merely the sanctification, of
life. This judgment upon Christianity is a

process of purification—the way to a transfigured life. It places man face to face with pure, naked reality. And that is well. The collapse of many historically sacred shrines may mean that man is approaching the true holy of holies, is nearer to God Himself. God does not need to be sanctified by man : He is holy in Himself alone.

For the world, the holiness of God is a judgment. This judgment extends to Christianity since Christianity is a part of history and has become infected with all of history's temptations and imperfections. Christianity as a human phenomenon, has been found to embody many of those mental and physical complexes which are revealed by modern psychopathology—sadism and masochism, the torture of one's self or of others. Sadism is evident even in Christian doctrine, for instance in that of endless punishment in hell. Here we need a process of spiritual cleansing. The judgment upon Christianity is going on in all phases of human life and culture. It is a judgment upon false monism and false dualism, upon extreme immanentism as well as extreme transcendentalism, upon the deification of human frailties and the degradation of human dignity. The world crisis is a judgment both from above and from beneath. The tragic conflict between Christianity and history is nothing new—it is eternal and in the process each judges the other.   History's judgment upon Christianity is its revelation of Christianity's failures in history. These failures indicate the points at which history has overcome Christianity instead of the reverse. History judges Christianity for having been conquered by history.   But on the other hand this defeat of Christianity turns into a judgment upon history.   The failure of Christianity is the failure of history as well.   This is more clearly evident now, than ever before.

It is in the social realm, which holds the centre of the stage in our time, that the judgment upon Christianity is passed, first of all.   It is undeniable that much of the true progress in social history is due to the open or indirect action of Christianity upon the human spirit : the abolition of slavery and serfdom, the recognition of freedom of conscience and of spiritual life are proofs of this. But instead of realizing these social reforms themselves, Christians have often left them to the hands of others, they have often even done injustice and consented to adapting higher spiritual values to the interests of the ruling class and the established order.   They have succeeded in producing a " bourgeois " Christianity.   And now the most merciless judgment is being passed upon this " bourgeois " Christianity, on every adaptation of Christianity to human, selfish, interests.

From the point of view of the workers,

Christianity has many unpleasant associations : Christians seem to have done everything possible to facilitate modern anti-religious propaganda among the labouring classes. The task of creating a more just and humane social order has fallen into the hands of anti-Christians, rather than Christians themselves. The divine has been torn apart from the human. This is the basis of all judgment, in the moral sphere, now being passed upon Christianity. All too often Christianity has been anti-human—has summoned men to fulfilment of the commandment to love God, without sufficient attention to the other, to love one's neighbour. Christians have drawn false moral conclusions from the doctrine of original sin, have denied man's creative capacity, and given their support to those forms of social order which gave rise to pressure and suffering, because they considered this good for sinful man. One of the worst examples of this deformation of Christian truth we find in relation to the virtue of obedience and humility. How often this has been distorted into humility in the face of evil, obedience to evil itself, a denial of personal conscience ! The religion of love and mercy has been transformed into a proclamation of cruel and relentless attitudes toward men. God's very idea of man as His image has been betrayed, as has that of the God-man and Divine-human life.

The judgment upon Christianity goes on in the cultural realm as well. All too often, as the result of a false concept of asceticism, Christianity has been hostile to creativity in culture : in philosophy, science, art, technics. It was only by second-thought, almost too late, that cultural creativity and social reform were sanctioned by Christianity, and hence human creative culture got out of Christian hands. The judgment is passed on Christian piety, on the old idea of asceticism. Asceticism was considered as an end, rather than a means, and so came to be anti-human, opposed to fullness of life and creativity. Monastic asceticism often led to a dessication of the human heart, and to a love of the abstract instead of the concrete. And to-day monasticism, both Eastern and Western, is passing through a grave crisis. The world needs a quite new form of monasticism, giving birth to a new piety. Christian piety all too often has seemed to be the withdrawal from the world and from men, a sort of transcendent egoism, the unwillingness to share the suffering of the world and man. It was not sufficiently infused with Christian love and mercy. It lacked human warmth. And the world has risen in protest against this sort of piety, as a refined form of egoism, as indifference to the world's sorrow. Against this protest only a reborn piety can stand. Care for the life of another, even material, bodily care, is spiritual in essence. Bread for myself is a material question : bread for my neighbour is a spiritual question.

This judgment on Christianity is being passed in the sphere of sex and love and marriage. The prevailing Christian teaching denied the meaning of love and called it accursed. And thus it came about that love, not in a baser, but in a higher form, began to be affirmed outside of, and even against Christianity. The bourgeois family, with its economic egoism and exclusiveness, was sanctified, but the intimate life of love departed from Christianity. The higher meaning of love was revealed by the Provençal troubadours and defended in prose and poetry. In this connection Christians lived in disagreement and dualism. Sex, and love and marriage were bound up with the family, rather than with personality, and personality could not endure this state of affairs. One of the surprising things in history is the relentless severity of Christianity in the matter of love, and its unusual leniency toward property, which it has sanctioned in its most evil forms.

A judgment is being passed on Christian theology, also, on the stifling rationalization of Christian truths and sacraments ; on the distortion of theological thought by social considerations, on the attribution of the most evil and sinful social relations between men to the relationships between God and man, God and His world. Only creative religious and philosophic thought can do the necessary work of cleansing, here, and defend the eternal truth of Christianity. Most of the deformation and clouding of Christianity has come about because man found it difficult to take in the full truth of God-manhood. Now man has turned to God and away from man, now toward man and away from God. But even when he turned away from humanity, man's evil human attitudes often prevailed in his relationship to God. The problem of Christian anthropology, the religious question of mankind, is the basic problem of our epoch. And only the fulness of Christian truth can fight successfully against dehumanization, and prevent the final destruction of man. The world tried to affirm man as against Christianity and arrived at a negation of man himself. And outside Christianity, or better, outside of Christ, there is no salvation for fallen man. To a renewed and transfigured Christianity man must now address himself for protection. This is the only defence for human dignity and freedom and creativity, for man's humanity to man. Only Christianity can create an inner society; what all the social movements produce is external.

III

The economic and political situations of the
world are terrible, even unbearable, but this is
true above all of its spiritual situation. The
very existence of spiritual life is in terrible danger,
the very possibility of its existence is threatened.
We live in an insane world. We have failed to
perceive that man has become insane. Because
of his thirst for life, his love of this world, man
has lost his spiritual and mental balance. The
world is again in the grip of the polydemonism
from which Christianity once rescued it. De-
Christianization led to dehumanization, and this
to insanity, since the very image of man is
darkened. Man has been laid open to every
sort of demoniac possession, of demonism; he
has become the prey of demonic, cosmic and
social forces. And man has thought his liberty
consisted in complete submission to just these
demonic forces.

Modern dehumanization puts man under the
sign of demoniac possession and loss of balance.
Our time is distinguished by the fact that this
demoniac possession is organized. When the
spirit ceases to control man's mental and corporeal
being, he loses his inner integrity and balance.
Cosmic and social forces rush in and organize
their possession by means of suggestion; as a

result of which man becomes possessed, either by the elementary, cosmic, telluric powers of the earth, of race, nation and sex, or by the elementary social forces of economic interest, money, class, social grouping, party. But spiritually, man is completely disorganized. He has lost his spiritual resistance to suggestion and possession. This is the loss of the very principle of personality, since personality is spirit, the spiritual resistance against all demoniac possession by impersonal cosmic or social forces. The work of the spirit is to illuminate man's physical and mental nature.

Only a mobilization of the spirit can be set up against modern collective insanity and demoniac possession, against modern polydemonism and idolatry. Social organization alone is powerless to struggle against this chaotic decay of the world and of man. The world threatens to become an organized and technicized chaos in which only the most terrible forms of idolatry and demonworship can live. Once again, man must return to monotheism, or else degenerate, be resolved into cosmic elements compulsorily organized into social collectives. The process of degeneration may go on in two directions, toward animalism and toward "machinism."

A new Christian piety must be revealed in our world. And upon this new Christian piety depends the fate of the world and that of man. It cannot be an abstract form, retirement from the world and from mankind: it must be a form of spiritual effort exerted over man and the world, labour for man and the world. It cannot permit human slavery to cosmic or social and technical forces. It calls man to a kingly role, and to creative work in the world. The new Christian man does not curse the world, neither does he condemn and anathematize the possessed and idolatrous. He shares the suffering of the world, bears in his body the tragedy of man. He strives to bring the liberating, spiritual element into all of human life. A personality which is strengthened and supported spiritually, cannot permit the powers of the world to divide its forces, can never permit itself to be possessed by demonic powers. Such a personality is not isolated and shut in upon itself, it is accessible to all universal meaning and open to all super-personal values.

This presents a very complex spiritual problem of relationship between the personal and the super-personal, a problem of personality entering into communal relationships, which is something quite other than personality becoming non-personal. The new piety is the road not only from the world and man to God, but the reverse, from God to man, descent as well as ascent, that is, the realization of the fulness of Divine-human truth, the truth of the God-man realized in life. In the old forms of Christian piety love of God often meant lack of love for man, repulsion from man, renunciation of the world as of something accursed. The only possible escape from this is in a new piety in which love of God will be love for man as well, and where freedom from the powers of this world will at the same time mean love for all of God's creation, a religion in which man's spiritual life will be not merely a process of attaining salvation, but creative in the world, as well. This does not mean a renunciation of asceticism, but only a new understanding of it, where the ascetic will be free from elements hostile to true life, and from what may be called religious nihilism.

Christianity is above all else a religion of love and liberty, but just because of this, the future is not determined by blind fate, either for good or for evil. Hence we move forward toward a tragic conflict. The new Christianity must re-humanize man and society, culture and the world. But for Christianity this process of humanization is something not merely human; it is Divine-human, of the nature of the God-man. Only in Divine-humanity, in the Body of Christ, can man be saved. Otherwise he will be torn to pieces by demonic forces, by the demons of hatred and malice.

This problem of man takes precedence over that of society or of culture, and here man is to be considered, not in his inner spiritual life, not as an abstract spiritual being, but as an integral being, as a being social and cosmic, as well. A new day is dawning for Christianity in the world. Only a form of Socialism, which unites personality and the communal principle, can satisfy Christianity. The hour has struck when, after terrible struggle, after an unprecedented de-Christianization of the world and its passage through all the results of that process, Christianity will be revealed in its pure form. Then it will be clear what Christianity stands for and what it stands against. Christianity will again become the only and the final refuge of man. And when the purifying process is finished, it will be seen that Christianity stands for man and for humanity, for the value and dignity of personality, for freedom, for social justice, for the brotherhood of men and of nations, for enlightenment, for the creation of a new life. And it will be clear that only Christianity stands for these things. The judgment upon Christianity is really judgment upon the betrayal of Christianity, upon its distortion and defilement and the justice of this is that of judgment upon the fallen world and its sinful history. But the true and final renaissance will probably begin in the world only after the elementary, everyday problems of human existence are solved for all peoples and nations, after bitter human need and the economic slavery of man have been finally conquered. Only then may we expect a new and more powerful revelation of the Holy Spirit in the world.

ANN ARBOR PAPERBACKS / *reissues of works of enduring merit*

The University of Michigan Press   Ann Arbor